ENOCH POWELL

The Man and his Thinking

ENOCH POWELL

The Man and his Thinking

T. E. UTLEY

WILLIAM KIMBER

6 QUEEN ANNE'S GATE, LONDON, S.W.1

First published in 1968 by
WILLIAM KIMBER & CO. LIMITED
6 Queen Anne's Gate, London, S.W.1

© T. E. Utley, 1968
SBN 7183 0131 5

MADE AND PRINTED IN GREAT BRITAIN BY PURNELL & SONS, LTD.
PAULTON (SOMERSET) AND LONDON

'I had to prepare the mind of the country, and . . . to educate our party.'

—*Benjamin Disraeli,*
Edinburgh, 1867

'And yet England is not as Nineveh and Tyre, nor as Rome, nor as Spain. Herodotus relates how the Athenians, returning to their city after it had been sacked and burnt by Xerxes and the Persian army, was astonished to find, alive and flourishing in the midst of the blackened ruins, the sacred olive tree, the native symbol of their country. So we today at the heart of a vanished empire, and the fragments of demolished glory, seem to find, like one of her own oak trees, standing and growing, the sap still rising from her ancient roots to meet the spring, England herself.'

—*Enoch Powell, Royal Society of*
St. George, 22nd April, 1964

Contents

Preface

This is not a biography of Enoch Powell, the time for which has happily not arrived. It is not, either, an exhaustive and scholarly study of his political and economic philosophy. It is an attempt to assess the significance of a phenomenon which, I believe, will disturb the peace of the Tory Party, for better or for worse, for many years to come.

I am extremely grateful to Mr. Powell for permission to quote many of his speeches, to Mr. John Biffen, M.P., for much valuable criticism throughout, and to Mr. Michael Harrington, diplomatic correspondent of the *Glasgow Herald*, for detailed and inestimable help with the chapter on defence. Above all, I am grateful to my assistant, Miss Frances Hill, for having assembled and read to me the material on which this book is based, for having typed the manuscript and corrected the proofs and for an incessant flood of criticism, the more valuable for having been made from a political standpoint wholly different from my own and vehemently different from that of my subject. No one but I can properly be held responsible for any of the opinions expressed in this book.

T.E.U.

ENOCH POWELL

The Man and his Thinking

I

The Speech

AN area meeting of the Conservative Political Centre is, in its nature, a somewhat undramatic occasion. The C.P.C. was a brainchild of R. A. Butler in the years immediately following the calamitous Conservative defeat of 1945. Its function was to convey and, if possible, to justify the impression that the Conservative Party had recaptured the intellectual initiative; or, in other words, that it was perfectly possible to be literate, rational, well-informed and a Tory.

For this purpose, the country was covered by a network of institutions dedicated to political education —to the instruction of the faithful in the history and the subtlety of Tory principles. It was all part of what Butler christened 'the two-way movement of ideas', a system under which the political élite which rules the Conservative party should be constantly refreshed by the inspirations and meditations of the more reflective sections of the rank and file which, in turn, would benefit from frank and lucid communication with their leaders.

A C.P.C. area meeting is attended by worthy provincial Conservatives with a taste for intellectual exercise. It is not, compulsorily, a private occasion, but its atmosphere is intended to be intimate. It does not normally provide a forum for major political speeches, or, indeed, for speeches intended to have any immediate impact on events. It is essentially an opportunity for philosophising; those who go to it are meant to emerge nourished rather than equipped for battle. The Press is not excluded, but it often finds the proceedings unworthy of report or of anything but the briefest mention, although, as a matter of fact, the year before Sir Keith Joseph had used this same meeting to launch a policy statement on housing which was subsequently published in full.

It was to precisely such a meeting in the Midland Hotel at Birmingham that Enoch Powell gave, on April 20th, a speech which dominated political conversation in Britain for at least a month, which changed the public reputation of the speaker almost beyond recognition and which was treated by some serious political commentators as a turning-point in Britain's political affairs.

Some inkling that the occasion was unusual was provided by the presence of television cameras and of a remarkably large contingent of Press reporters. However, the subject—immigration—was topical in view of the fact that the Government's Race Relations Bill was to be debated the following Tuesday. What is more, it was of crucial interest to a West Midlands audience, and it was one on which Enoch Powell had already given strong expression to his views on several occasions. All this might explain an unusual amount of public interest in what would normally have been regarded as a semi-academic discourse.

Certainly, there is little evidence that the immediate audience thought the speech in any way extraordinary. The Press reported that Powell received a standing ovation when he left the hall, but this is not entirely true. On arriving, he told the Chairman of the meeting, Reginald Ayer, Member for a Birmingham constituency and one of the Tory Party's Whips, that he had to leave early in order to give a B.B.C. interview. When a reasonable time had been given to questions, therefore, and a courteous vote of thanks had been moved, Ayer rose to say that the speaker must now leave in order to keep another engagement. In keeping with ordinary convention, the audience also rose while the speaker left the hall. There was a substantial round of applause, and at question time, no sign of hostility to the line which Powell had taken. Those present thought the speech characteristically stimulating. It was addressed to matters which closely affected their lives and it expressed their own opinions about them in language more vivid than politicians normally use. I am credibly told that no-one there, including the Whip in the chair, had the remotest idea that this was a specially note-worthy occasion, or one likely to provoke any kind of crisis in the Conservative Party.

The gratifying response from the media was due largely to the acuteness of a B.B.C. Television editor in Birmingham. Controversy has since raged about the extent to which Powell himself went out of his way to publicise his speech, and about the extent to which, in so doing, he carefully avoided using any channels which might have involved giving his colleagues in the Shadow Cabinet foreknowledge of what he intended to say. The facts are these: the Conservative Central Office maintains a Press Department for the purpose of helping Conservative M.P.s to get the maximum publicity for their utterances. It is normal but in no way obligatory for a Tory member to use the services of this department. Obviously, the department itself exercises no censorship on what it distributes, though it would not be unnatural or unseemly for its head, Mr. Gerald O'Brien, to draw the attention of the Party leader to any speech which seemed likely to prove of major importance to the Party's fortunes in the country.

A speaker who intended to deviate from the strict Party line or to fly a kite of his own which had not received specific approval from the leadership sometimes refrains from exposing Party officials to the embarrassment of distributing a handout. Powell, the author of many controversial speeches, has, I am told, shown this restraint on more occasions than one. Certainly, he sent no text or summary of his speech at Birmingham to the Central Office's Press Department. On the other hand, he sent several copies to the West Midlands Conservative Area Office for distribution to the local Press, and with them an instruction that a copy should also be dispatched to the Press Association which serves the National Press.

It is evident and significant that the loyal party workers of the Midland Area Office found nothing at

all extraordinary in the text of Powell's lecture. The
B.B.C.'s Birmingham office, however, instantly identified it as an event worthy of full sound and television
coverage. The journalists also reached the same conclusion without a moment's hesitation, and the I.T.V.
News Service rapidly followed suit.

Mr. O'Brien of the Central Office's Press Department was at the time on holiday in Oxford. Early on
the morning of Powell's speech, however, he had
occasion to ring up the Editor of the *News of the World*
to discuss with him the arrangements for an article on
race relations due to appear from Mr. Heath the following morning. The Editor warned him that this judicious piece would almost certainly be overshadowed
by a 'shaker of a speech' to be delivered by Powell
at Birmingham that afternoon—a judgment which was
proved overwhelmingly right.

Powell was interviewed by the B.B.C. on its six
o'clock newsreel on Saturday night, extracts from his
speech were broadcast on the B.B.C.'s and I.T.V.'s
television news services the same evening, and a large
part of the sound programme 'The Weekend at One'
was devoted to him. His speech was the lead in every
national Sunday paper the next day, and was the
subject of impassioned comment then and the day after.

His modest arrangements for local publicity had
yielded an astonishing harvest.

The Powell family is well known for its determined
domesticity and for the particular importance it attaches
to keeping the world at bay on Sundays. After his
speech, Powell returned to his house in Wolverhamp-

ton. On Sunday after church, he and his wife drove
their daughters to a riding school and spent the rest
of the day in relaxed family pursuits. He followed his
almost invariable custom of not reading the Sunday
newspapers.

His first intimation of the interest aroused by what
he had said at Birmingham was a telephone call from
Mr. Heath at nine o'clock in the evening dismissing
him from the Shadow Cabinet. He was, he professes,
wholly astonished at the stir he had caused.

Mr. Heath read Powell's speech for the first time
in the form in which it was reported in the Sunday
press. By lunch-time he had summoned the Chief Whip,
Mr. William Whitelaw, from Cumberland and himself
driven up from Broadstairs to his flat in Albany. By
nine o'clock his mind was made up, and an hour later
he publicly announced his decision to sack Powell for
a speech which was 'racialist in tone and liable to
exacerbate racial tensions'.

Mr. Jeremy Thorpe, Leader of the Liberal Party,
went so far as to suggest that there was a *prima facie*
case for prosecuting Powell for incitement to racial
prejudice, and Mr. Ted Leadbitter, Labour member
for Hartlepools, referred the speech to the Attorney
General with a view to such prosecution.

A distinguished Shadow Cabinet colleague of
Powell, and one by no means noted for progressive
inclinations, heard the B.B.C.'s report of the speech
on the television news on Saturday night. He was
instantly moved to ring up the Chief Whip in Cumberland and recommend him to watch the I.T.V. news.
Mr. Whitelaw, having watched the news, instantly

rang back to say that the speech was 'a shocker' and
sure to cause a crisis in the Party.

From all this certain facts emerge clearly: in the
West Midlands, Powell's speech appeared to be a
vigorous though not particularly shocking or even particularly original contribution to a familiar debate. To
almost all the political and journalistic establishment
elsewhere, it was instantly apparent that it was dynamite. Friends, enemies and neutrals all immediately
recognised it as a challenge either to the authority of
Mr. Heath and the Shadow Cabinet or even to the
whole politics of consensus on the racial issue.

To what extent was this challenge deliberate? Powell
has repeatedly maintained that it was not. The mystery
that remains to be solved, however, is how a politician
of his experience and astuteness can have failed to
foresee—whatever people on the spot thought—if not
the rift with his Shadow Cabinet colleagues which
ensued, then at least the public uproar which his speech
caused.

Powell was throughout convinced that his speech
was wholly consistent with the doctrine of his Party.
May he not in retrospect have underestimated the extent to which he realised at the time (half consciously,
perhaps) that by dramatising that doctrine and drawing
out what he thought to be its ultimate implications, he
was making an important impact on politics and taking
a decisive step in his political career?

But if so, what kind of a step was it?

To understand this it is necessary to look at the
speech itself. In several ways it was wholly typical of

the speaker. Its structure is rigorously logical, its style sternly academic but showing signs of intense and intensely controlled passion.

Powell starts with the general and proceeds to the particular. He begins with broad reflections on the two neglected roles of statesmanship—the task of anticipating by present action evils which will become real or extreme only in the future and the historic duty of the M.P. to provide a mouthpiece for his constituents' grievances. Before getting down to these tasks, incidentally, he betrays a vivid sense of the reaction he is likely to evoke in some quarters by using these words: 'I can already hear the chorus of execration. How dare I say such a horrible thing? How dare I stir up trouble and inflame feelings. . . .'

What gave the speech its special flavour, however, was the technique which Powell chose to employ of allowing his constituents or their friends to speak for themselves through direct quotation. One of these quotations—an extract from a letter written by a lady in Northumberland but purporting to describe events in Wolverhampton—was seized on by his critics as proof positive that Powell was a racialist.

It told the story of alleged persecution of an old and impecunious lady by her black neighbours, and included the description of such amenities as the placing of human excrement in her letter-box. It also contained a reference, widely deemed to be offensive, to 'charming, wide-grinning piccaninnies'. Again, the words were not Powell's but those of his correspondent. He could rationally claim that by reproducing these striking passages he was not expressing his own feeling or even reporting his own observations but simply providing evidence of the strength of feeling among the white inhabitants of the Midlands, a feeling which statesmanship must take into account in shaping policy.

The hard core of Powell's argument depended upon one statistic supplied by the spokesman of the Registrar General's office. It was that in fifteen or twenty years there would be 3½ million Commonwealth immigrants and their descendants in the United Kingdom. The value of this statistic was at least disputable. It was based on an answer given to Sir Cyril Osborne in the House of Commons in June 1967. Sir Cyril had asked what the coloured population of the country would be in 1975 and 1985 on the assumption that immigration continued at the rate at which it was then proceeding, and on the assumption also that the known immigrant birthrate would not diminish.

Powell in his speech gave his own reasons for believing that at any rate as far ahead as 1985 the two assumptions would be valid. This view, however, is strongly contested: for instance, in October, 1967 Mr. David Ennals of the Home Office, bearing in mind the declining rate of immigration and the statistics about fertility, computed that in 1985 the coloured population would be nearer 2½ million. The Commonwealth Immigrants' Act of 1968, by cutting down the hitherto unrestricted inflow of Kenyan Asians to only 1,500 a year, ensured a further reduction. The truth is that those who dabble in this kind of prediction are dabbling in the completely imponderable.

In order to enforce his argument Powell undoubtedly

chose the highest estimate available. It was almost
certainly a false estimate.

Powell showed some awareness of the criticism to
which his figures might be subjected by an almost
parenthetic remark in his speech. 'Let no-one suppose,'
he declared, 'that the flow of dependents will automatically tail off. On the contrary, even at the present
admission rate of only 5,000 a year by voucher, there
is sufficient for a further 25,000 dependents per annum
ad infinitum. . . .' Three and a half million by 1985,
however, remained the basis of his argument. A man
of different temperament, equipped with so strong a
case as Powell, might have thought it prudent to under-
estimate, rather than to expose himself to the charge of
exaggeration.

What is most remarkable, however, is the extreme
generality and unoriginality of the practical conclusions
about future policy to which this analysis led Powell.
On the future level of immigration, he concluded that
'nothing will suffice but that the total inflow for settlement should be reduced at once to negligible proportions, and that the necessary legislative and administrative measures be taken without delay'. On the case
of dependents, he stated, philosophically, 'It can be
no part of any policy that existing families should be
kept divided; but there are two directions in which
families can be reunited, and if our former and present
immigration laws have brought about the division of
families, albeit voluntary or semi-voluntarily, we ought
to be prepared to arrange for them to be re-united in
their countries of origin.'

So far Powell's recommendations have not gone

much further in principle, than the declared policies
of his Party. His leader, writing in the *News of the
World* on the very day on which Powell's speech was
reported, called for 'the most stringent control of future
immigration'. Powell had spoken of reducing immigration to 'negligible proportions'. The difference
between them, if there is one, is certainly one of degree
and style. The Tory party had already committed itself
to the principle that future immigrants, before being
admitted, should be obliged to state how many dependents they had who might eventually wish to follow
them. It was also committed to the view that generous
financial help should be given to any immigrant who
wanted to return to his own country. Powell might well
claim that, in his own vivid way, he was 'towing the
Party line'. Certainly, he could claim to be doing no
more than putting the most stringent possible interpretation on his Party's commitments.

What Powell cannot be acquitted of is the charge
of skirting round the one major moral dilemma which
has perplexed the Tories in their consideration of this
problem for the last year or so.

It is one thing to recommend a drastic reduction in
the number of immigrants to whom work vouchers
should be granted. It is also morally easy to refuse
work vouchers to immigrants who are likely to bring a
large number of dependents in their train. It is quite
another for a party which is fond of preaching the
sanctity of the family and the honouring of pledges to
assert that immigrants already established here (who
came on the assumption that their relations would be
allowed to follow them) should be told that in future

they are forbidden to bring dependents over. That dilemma cannot be solved by suggesting that the immigrants should go home and be helped finaniaclly to do so. Suppose they decline to go home: are they to be deported? Or are they to be allowed to remain only on condition that they accept continued separation from their families? Powell's words suggest that it is this second alternative which he is recommending, but a certain amount of ambiguity is allowed to remain.

It is the second stage of Powell's argument which exemplifies most clearly the defects of this speech and one of his recurring weaknesses as an orator—a tendency to press arguments not, as is often said, to their logical conclusions but to conclusions which, although expressed in language which suggests remorseless rigour of thought, in fact defy logic. Here again Powell's thesis was essentially that of the majority of his Party. He held that the Government's Race Relations Bill designed to prevent discrimination in such matters as housing, employment and the granting of credit facilities would exacerbate rather than diminish racial conflict and create personal injustices worse than those which it would rectify. Clearly, these are respectable and tenable propositions, but consider the manner in which Powell formulates them: 'The third element of the Conservative Party's policy is that all who are in this country as citizens should be equal before the law and that there shall be no discrimination or difference made between them by public authority. . . . This does not mean that the immigrant and his descendants should be elevated into a privileged or special class or that the citizen should be denied his right to discriminate in the management of his own affairs between one fellow-citizen and another or that he should be subjected to imposition as to his reasons and motives for behaving in one lawful manner rather than another.'

The first assumption which is tacitly made in this tightly packed passage is that anti-discrimination laws automatically create privileged classes. To the unconverted this must seem a startling paradox, since such laws, in form at any rate, prohibit discrimination by blacks against whites as firmly as discrimination by whites against blacks. If in practice they are more likely to be invoked by coloured immigrants than by white inhabitants, the reason is that at this moment the white population is better placed to exercise discrimination than is the immigrant population—a fact which it would plainly not suit Powell's argument to emphasise. As a result an essential stage in that argument is omitted.

Then again to suggest that the new law will subject the citizen to inquisitions about his reasons 'for behaving in one lawful manner rather than another' is to suggest the absurd. Since discrimination on racial grounds will become unlawful, the inquisitions will be directed not to establishing the reasons for pieces of lawful behaviour, but for establishing whether illegal behaviour has taken place. A speaker of Powell's intellectual gifts and particular style cannot expect immunity from criticism which would seem pedantic when applied to others.

The point which Powell is trying to make is one of

substance. It is that it is virtually impossible to preclude discrimination in the sale of a house or the granting of a loan without running the risk of forbidding legitimate exercises of private judgment which have nothing to do with racial prejudice. It is arguable that preserving the rights of private judgment in such matters is more important than abolishing discrimination. Powell should be the first to acknowledge that politics is a choice of evils. His case was gratuitously weakened by his determination not to recognise the existence of one of the evils. This becomes flagrantly apparent in his astonishingly one-sided assertion: 'The discrimination and the deprivation, the sense of alarm and resentment, lies not with the immigrant population but with those among whom they have come and are still coming.'

To achieve what was plainly a dramatic purpose, Powell is finally driven to press his arguments far beyond the limits of the evidence he has quoted. 'Now we are seeing the growth of positive forces acting against integration, of vested interests in the preservation and sharpening of racial and religious differences, with a view to the exercise of actual domination, first over fellow-immigrants and then over the rest of the population.'

As a description of the Black Power movement this is no doubt fair, but Powell makes no specific reference to that movement. Instead he triumphantly cites the witness of a left-wing Socialist and anti-racialist, Mr. Stonehouse, to prove his point. Censuring the Sikh community for insisting on wearing their turbans when working on the municipal bus service in Wolverhampton,

Stonehouse had said, 'To claim special communal rights (or should one say rites?) leads to a dangerous fragmentation within society.' Plainly, a racial group which aspires to domination must first segregate itself from the rest of the community, but it does not necessarily follow that a racial group which thus segregates itself aspires to domination.

As an exhibition of the famous 'steam roller intellect', the speech has serious blemishes. In its handling of the statistics, in the telescoped and emotive form of much of the argument, it appears as a political act rather than a contribution to debate. What is more the practical conclusions which it is intended to sustain are far from being precisely defined; hence, the ease with which Powell has since been able to maintain that he has said nothing to which his Party has not already agreed.

It would be equally wrong to dismiss the speech as a piece of demagogy. It was manifestly not intended to inflame the crowd nor would it be at all likely to provoke acts of racial violence. The habit of attributing every racial brawl which has taken place in any part of Britain since April 20th to the contents of Powell's speech is simply silly. It was the political establishment and not least the establishment of the Conservative Party which Powell in fact provoked.

Powell is emphatically not a racialist in the only intelligible meaning of that expression—one who believes in the natural inferiority of some races to others and in the justice of legal and social arrangements designed to register that inferiority. He may fairly be described as a nationalist in the sense that he believes that a degree of cultural homogeneity is necessary to the stability of society. To that extent he believes (and who can rationally gainsay him?) that the cultural and racial composition of the community and the speed with which that composition changes are proper concerns of government.

To neglect these concerns, he is passionately convinced, is to endanger the survival of the State, the security of the rule of law and the sacred convention of equal respect for different cultural groups within the State's jurisdiction. Had they been stated thus abstractly, Powell's beliefs might have been dismissed as a collection of tired platitudes. As it was, his dramatic rendering of them turned British politics upside down within twenty-four hours.

What remains to be considered is why this moment was chosen for what was evidently a carefully if subconsciously planned explosion. From 1962 onwards Commonwealth immigration was a subject of recurrent interest in British politics. In that year, Mr. Macmillan's Government imposed limits on the rights of citizens of the Commonwealth to enter this country. Many Conservatives opposed this retreat from the principle of equal British citizenship under the crown, and the Labour Party opposed it strongly.

Since then, the trend in all parties has been towards an increasing recognition of the fact that Commonwealth immigration into Britain constitutes a serious social problem. Labour, having made capital out of the view that the Conservative Party is racialist, has steadily retreated from its original position of unqualified support for the view that any citizen of the

Commonwealth should be allowed to settle in this country. The defeat of Mr. Patrick Gordon Walker at the General Election of 1964 and his subsequent defeat at a by-election shortly afterwards, even though he had been appointed Foreign Secretary in the meantime, were attributed largely to the immigration issue. It became apparent that no Government that wished to survive could ignore this issue, and Labour maintained a system of immigration control imposed by the Tories in 1962.

One loophole in this system, however, was the offer of British passports to Kenyan Asians, who wished to emigrate from Kenya, made by Britain as part of the arrangements for the institution of Kenyan independence. As the racialist tendencies of the Kenyan Government became increasingly evident, this right was increasingly used, and a group of Conservatives led by Mr. Duncan Sandys and supported by Powell had strongly demanded throughout the second half of 1967 that something should be done to stop this influx of Asian immigrants.

In February of this year, the Government yielded to the demand, imposing strict control on the immigration of Kenyan Asians and of all holders of British passports who could not establish that one or both of their parents had lived in this country. This measure was accompanied by a stricter control of immigration in general. It aroused extreme opposition both from the Socialist left and from those Conservatives who felt that it involved a breach of obligations deliberately undertaken.

The Conservative Party did not oppose this Com-

monwealth Immigration Bill. To this extent, Powell
had already won an important part of his case. The
Government and the Opposition were both alive as
never before to the dangers of unlimited immigration.
The Conservative Party's official view was that immigration should be strictly controlled, that immigrants
should not be allowed to enter the country until they
had stated how many dependents they might bring
with them and that every possible financial facility
should be given to them to return to their own countries. By April 1968 a politician with Powell's views
on immigration might have thought that he was doing
rather well.

Similarly, in relation to the question of what, if any,
special legal arrangements should be made for the
protection of immigrants in this country, the views
expressed by Powell in his speech had made extraordinary headway in the Conservative Party. As soon
as it was known that the Government was resolved to
introduce a second Race Relations Bill extending legal
protection to housing, employment and credit facilities,
it became clear that the Conservative Party was deeply
divided about what its response to this Bill should
be.

On the whole question of immigration, the Conservative Party suffers an acute and perennial *crise de
conscience*. Both its liberal and its imperialist wings have
special reasons for supporting the concept of the multi-
racial society. Many Conservatives, for one reason or
the other, were reluctant to oppose any Bill extending
the legal protection afforded to immigrants. Mr. Heath,
for liberal rather than imperialistic reasons, was

rumoured to favour such legislation. Sir Edward Boyle was known to favour it with some degree of passion. The problem of how the Conservative Party should react to the new Race Relations Bill therefore closely affected Party unity.

Mr. Quintin Hogg, official spokesman of the Party on Home Affairs and therefore the Shadow Minister chiefly responsible for immigration, is a man of strong liberal instincts and equally strong Conservative convictions. As a lawyer, he has an extreme dislike of legislation which is not enforceable or which cannot be enforced with any certainty of impartiality. From the first he disliked the Government's Bill; he was equally concerned that in withholding its support the Conservative Party should not appear to favour discrimination. For this reason, and because of the need to preserve unity in the face of an issue over which consciences were deeply divided, his first instinct was to favour a free vote on the Bill. The suggestion was rejected on the understandable ground that the Conservative Party ought not to seem to be side-tracking a question now recognised to be of major public importance. Accordingly, the Shadow Cabinet set out to achieve a consensus.

The method was that of a reasoned amendment to the Bill, implying sympathy with its aims but belief that the means proposed for achieving them would be ineffective and harmful. The terms of the amendment were drafted with some difficulty, and Powell was one of the members of the Shadow Cabinet entrusted with the task of devising them. The compromise, it appears, was completely satisfactory to him. He did not object to it in the Shadow Cabinet and, after his speech at Birmingham, he voted for it in the Commons.

There can be little doubt that this decision of the Shadow Cabinet was a signal victory for what may roughly be described as the right wing. The extent of this victory was soon marked by the resignation from the Party of the ex-M.P. Humphrey Berkeley who had come over a period of years to symbolise the Tory left wing. In a long letter of resignation to the Party Leader, which elicited an even longer reply, Berkeley complained of what he regarded as the increasingly racialist tendencies of the Conservatives evinced in their handling of the Rhodesian question and now in their approach to racial discrimination. Edward Heath was plainly deeply distressed at Berkeley's departure, a fact which confirmed many in the view that the Tory Leader is more concerned to preserve the loyalty of his left wing than that of his right wing. It seemed highly probable that Sir Edward Boyle, the principal representative of the left in the Shadow Cabinet, would defy the Party Whips to the extent of voting for the Race Relations Bill. Had Powell's speech not been made, the Party's handling of the Bill would almost certainly have been interpreted as proof that at long last Heath had been captured by the right and a gulf created between him and those of his 'progressive minded' supporters to whom he had hitherto been supposed to incline.

In the event, this triumph of the right was gratuitously thrown away. Powell's speech was the subject of a bitter, indeed often a hysterical, attack from large sections of the Press. *The Times*, in an almost frenzied leader, described it flatly as 'an evil speech'. There is little doubt also that it angered, perplexed and disturbed in various degrees almost all his colleagues in the Shadow Cabinet. Hogg reluctantly condemned it in the Commons debate as disloyal; an eminent colleague, who has often hunted with Powell in the past, declined to discuss it with me on the grounds that he was 'bitterly offended' by it. If the object of the exercise was to provoke the political establishment, it had achieved unqualified success.

In particular, it enabled Heath to do what the evidence suggests he would have gladly done at several points in the last two years—removed Powell from the Shadow Cabinet. Such action would have seriously and immediately weakened the Leader's position at any moment before the 21st of April. Powell's speech made it possible. What is more, the extent of his differences with the leadership completely obliterated the serious differences which had arisen between Heath and the Conservative left. Boyle, it is true, declined to vote for the Party's reasoned amendment to the Race Relations Bill, but he did not vote for the Bill either. Technically, Powell's friends might complain that a member of the Shadow Cabinet with left-wing inclinations had been allowed to defy the Party Whip with impunity, while Powell had been sacked for supporting the party line. Nothing could be more obvious, however, than the fact that Powell's speech was a direct affront to the leadership in a sense in which Boyle's abstention was not. What persuaded Powell at this moment to deliver such an affront?

c

The explanation must go back to Powell's decision to accept a Shadow Office under Sir Alec Douglas Home after the Tory defeat in 1964. Powell, it will be recalled, had objected strongly to the processes by which Home was chosen as leader of the Conservative Party on the resignation of Macmillan in 1963 and had accordingly declined to serve under the new Prime Minister. The complex reasoning which led to this decision affords an interesting clue to the character and opinions of Powell, a clue which must later be investigated.

When the Tories went into Opposition, the question was whether Powell would heal the breach with his Leader, a man not given to bearing grudges, or would prefer a role of splendid isolation on the back benches, in which he might uninhibitedly recommend changes in the philosophy and policy of the Party. There can be no doubt that he considered both possibilities carefully. At one time he seemed inclined to prefer the back benches, arguing that a place in the front lines of the Opposition in the first phase of a new Parliament was particularly vulnerable. His argument was that a new Opposition almost invariably starts out on the wrong track, and that it might be better to influence Conservative policy from the rear before assuming any kind of official responsibility for its defence. 'Let the women and children go first!' was the charmingly ironic phrase in which he expressed the view.

In the event, however, Powell decided to accept Home's proposal and became spokesman on transport. Having refused office twice and resigned once, he may well have calculated that a third refusal would

confirm the deadly criticism already privately formulated by his former patron R. A. Butler that he
was 'a natural resigner'. He may also have legitimately
calculated that radical speeches on the reform of Tory
policy were likely to have more effect when delivered
by a Shadow Minister, whose services had been repeatedly proved to be indispensable, than by a back
bencher. The perennial danger overhanging Powell's
political career is the possibility that he may be classified as an eccentric or, at best, a philosopher with no
real interest in or ultimate capacity for political life.
That danger was diminished by his reappearance on
the front benches.

It is plain, however, that, by word and action,
Powell constantly made it clear to his Leader that he
did not regard membership of the Shadow Cabinet as
precluding him from the freest possible expression of
his political ideas. From the moment he left office in
1963, he was conscious of a clear mission—to destroy
the collectivist heresies to which he believed the Conservative Party had become a victim during its thirteen
years' rule. The Party had made false assumptions and
drawn false inferences from them. It was intellectually
confused and it was in need of a total redefinition of
its doctrines. Powell would make it his business to
expose these fallacies and to enable the Party to emerge
with a completely new sense of purpose and a completely new sense of its relationship to various sections
of the electorate.

Powell could be excused for not supposing that
there was any natural incompatibility between this
mission and membership of the Shadow Cabinet. The

concept of a Shadow Cabinet has no part in Britain's regular constitutional arrangements. The Labour Party, it is true, elects a small Parliamentary committee to govern its affairs when in opposition, and this committee becomes, in effect, the Shadow Cabinet.

No such system of election inhibits the Conservative Leader's choice of those colleagues upon whom he will principally depend when not in office. He seeks his council where he will, assigning particular roles to particular Members but in no way committing himself to them permanently or limiting his freedom of choice in selecting a Cabinet when he is returned to power. Under Churchill, for instance, the Shadow Cabinet was an extremely loose association, and it was widely said that the Leader could remember the names of its members only with difficulty. Certainly, membership of this loose association was never thought, until comparatively recent times, to impose any kind of obligation to conform in detail to declared Party policies.

Undoubtedly, however, the Shadow Cabinet has become increasingly formalised since in 1965 Heath became Leader of the Conservative Party. The new Leader's political experience had largely been gained as a Chief Whip of exemplary tact and diligence. He has brought a Whip's mentality to bear on the task of leadership. His Shadow Cabinet is highly organised and he has even developed Shadow Under-Secretaryships. Possibly because he is the first Conservative Leader to owe his position to a free election among back benchers (the electoral processes to which his predecessors were subjected were purely formal in character) he has been exceptionally sensitive to the least suggestion of criticism from his colleagues. He has looked with disfavour on speeches by Shadow Ministers which address themselves to matters outside the particular departmental responsibilities he has entrusted to them. When given a chance, he has scrutinised such speeches with some care before they were delivered and has frequently insisted that changes should be made to bring them more closely into line with official policy. He has not been loth to summon erring colleagues to his elegant flat in the Albany for what the Press describes as 'carpeting'. Early in his career as Leader, for example, he placed an unfavourable construction on a philosophical article of almost unfathomable obscurity by Angus Maude, then a Shadow Under-Secretary, and promptly relieved him of such minimal responsibilities as that Shadowy office confers.

Under such a Leader, Powell's evangelising mission was bound to present difficulties. Powell firmly, constantly and openly refused to be muzzled. His attitude, repeatedly confided in private, was that he intended to speak freely on all aspects of Conservative policy, indicating when he was and when he was not expressing the agreed view of the Party. So long as this freedom was allowed to him, he was prepared to belong to the Shadow Cabinet; it was for his Leader to decide how long that membership was tolerable.

As the years went by, relations between Powell and Heath became increasingly strained. Powell's speeches, mainly directed towards advocating the merits of a wholly or almost entirely free economy, seemed to Heath to be driving the Conservative Party too far and too fast along a dangerous road. Outright condemnations of incomes policies in any form and strongly implied criticisms of regionalism (Heath as Secretary of State for Trade had been charged by Home with the formulation of plans to help the underdeveloped regions of Britain) particularly rankled. Though on the platform Heath continued to affirm that Powell was making a most useful and stimulating contribution to thought, he did not trouble to conceal, even from journalists, his annoyance at Powell's aberrations. More than a year ago he was in the habit of saying that 'the less Enoch talks the better'.

Even in his own sphere, now that of defence, Powell advocated policies far in advance of the Conservative consensus. There is evidence that his belief in the abandonment of commitments East of Suez and the concentration of Britain's defence effort in Europe was in fact pleasing to the Leader. It was, however, calculated to outrage the substantial imperialist wing of the Tory Party and to deprive the Opposition of a stick with which to beat the Government when Mr. Wilson himself was forced to start a rapid retreat from engagements overseas.

Powell, as spokesman on defence, succeeded to his own satisfaction in both condemning the Government for its Little Englandism and in keeping his own principles intact, but the complicated gymnastics involved in this exercise were not everywhere understood or admired. On his part, Powell certainly formed the impression that Heath had let him down over defence.

Neither man is gifted with the capacity for relaxed social intercourse. Powell is by nature combative but rigidly self-controlled. He has a taste for intellectual battles and an ability to wage them with the emotional detachment and fundamental good humour of a don. Heath is a sensitive introvert to whom personal affection and loyalty do not seem easily to combine with strong intellectual disagreement.

Powell has achieved a style of oratory which marks him out as one of the most forceful of present-day parliamentarians, though it does not quite place him in the historic ranks of the great. As a speaker, the most that can be said of Heath is that his patient and undistinguished discourses give his audiences the impression that he is a man who understands his subject; it would be too much to say that, when he sits down, his audiences also understand it.

Powell's reputation has rested in recent years on the sustained talent for exaggeration; Heath's on an infinite gift for understatement. Powell more easily hits the headlines than his Leader does. It would be a bold man who altogether rejected the idea that Heath's decision to dismiss him on April 21st had nothing whatever to do with the interest aroused in that Sunday's papers by Powell's speech and the almost complete neglect accorded to an article on the same subject by Heath in the *News of the World*.

Any surviving doubt about the inevitability of the clash between these two men must be dispelled by the terms of the quite extraordinary letter which, in response to his dismissal, Powell wrote to Heath. After a protestation of his faith that Heath would one day be Prime Minister and 'perhaps even a great one', he went on to point out, with gracious patronage, one defect which he hoped time would remove, 'the impression you often give of playing down and even unsaying policies and views which you hold and believe to be right, for fear of clamour from some section of the Press or public'. It would be hard to imagine a letter more likely to create a permanent breach between two men or a criticism of Heath more precisely calculated to injure his public reputation.

The breach, then, was inevitable. As to its timing, there seems no reason to suppose that it was deliberately designed by Powell. His campaign for the reform of the Conservative Party has proceeded from the first under its own momentum. He has from the first been resolved that it should take precedence over the retention of his post in the Shadow Cabinet and even over the maintenance of civil relations with his colleagues. He would stay so long as they wanted him; it was for them to decide. In a sense the martyrdom of dismissal —on an issue on which he might claim to be doing no more than zealously upholding the Party line—was preferable to yet another resignation.

From this breach Powell has derived certain clear advantages and disadvantages. On the debit side, he is now effectively removed from direct influence on the strategy and tactics of his Party. He has abandoned the Shadow Cabinet men who, on the whole, are at best intrigued by his ideas and profoundly suspicious of their political value, and at the worst are dedicatedly hostile to everything for which he stands. As will be seen later, Powell's presence on the front benches had been largely responsible for a slow but perceptible evolution of official Tory policy in the Powellite direction.

At the same time, Powell has bewildered the Tory back benches including some who had become increasingly disposed to admire him. In 1965 fifteen members were prepared to stand up and be counted as Powell's supporters in the election to the Party leadership. That faithful nucleus had shown some tendency to expand, though never in the context of a possible and immediate direct challenge to Heath. Though Powell had alienated comparatively few back benchers by his immigration speech, he has increased the atmosphere of doubt and mystery by which to some extent he has always been surrounded in the Commons. Powell is an assiduous parliamentarian with a strong romantic devotion to Westminster, but he is not and never has been a clubable parliamentarian. He does not sit in the smoking room, his contacts with his colleagues are determinedly brief and business-like. He is on record as saying that there are few close and permanent friendships in politics, and this natural reserve has been markedly increased in the last two years by a determination not to be regarded as trying to build up any parliamentary alliance or conspiracy against his Leader.

In Parliament, therefore, Powell's position has on balance been weakened. In the country, it has been improved to a positively revolutionary extent. Most of the speeches in which the Powellite position has been dramatically outlined during the last few years were addressed to the country rather than the Commons. They have achieved a substantial though not a glittering success. Powell has a surprising and not easily explicable knack of appealing to working-class audiences, particularly in the Midlands. He is also meat and drink to the journalists. Among a section of the politically articulate young, particularly in the universities, he has fervent admirers. It was for instance his friends at St. Andrew's University who had printed, long before the immigration speech, the handful of car stickers which affirm that 'Powell Talks Sense'. The reference, then, was to his advocacy of laissez-faire principles and his fiercely ironic denunciations of bureaucracy.

It must have been painfully apparent to him, however, by April of this year that reasoned expositions of the fallacies involved in Prices and Incomes policy, humorous assaults on the questionnaires sent to hotel keepers by the Board of Trade and learned dissertations on the need for a floating pound were not likely to make him into a popular political hero. Certainly, his advocacy of withdrawal from foreign commitments is not the kind of aphrodisiac to which Tory-minded working-men traditionally respond. Immigration is the one note which Powell has struck in the hearts of the people.

The evidence shows conclusively that Powell's Birmingham speech accomplished a drastic transformation in his whole political reputation. There can, indeed, be few precedents for such a transformation. In a Gallup Poll taken in April (before the speech) one per cent of those questioned said that they would like Powell to succeed to the leadership if Heath went. Maudling, Home, Macleod, Hogg all decisively beat him. At a Gallup Poll taken early in May Powell had leapt to the top of the runners-up with twenty-four per cent. Within a few days of his speech, he had received

105,000 letters of congratulation and been the object of favourable demonstrations by dockers, Smithfield meat porters and Midland factory workers. He had even been the object of a number of threats of assassination, a comparatively rare distinction in British politics.

Powellism, or at any rate something thought to be Powellism, had ceased to be the eccentric profession of a few sophisticates and become a strong popular movement.

It is an almost invariable rule of Conservative politics in Britain that the party leadership is the reward for a diligent cultivation of opinion at Westminster; indeed, it is generally conferred by a comparatively small political oligarchy. Attempts to appeal over the heads of that oligarchy, however, are also a recurring theme in Conservative politics. It has been the dream of many Conservative politicians to forge a genuinely democratic Tory movement, to rise to power on a wave of evangelical enthusiasm, to present themselves not in the characteristically Conservative role of safe men with their feet on the ground but in the role of prophets expressing the native sentiments of simple people in vigorous and intelligible language. Such was the ambition of Lord Randolph Churchill and that of Joseph Chamberlain. It is a kind of ambition which is particularly repellent to the ordinary run of Conservative politicians, who prefer to think of themselves as divinely commissioned to control rather than to express popular enthusiasm. Over and again, however, the Conservative Party has been revived by movements of this kind and to their exasperation, the more con-

ventional Conservative leaders have been forced to try
and contain these movements within the Party's framework. Much of Baldwin's political career, for example,
was devoted to the task of trying to contain and control
Chamberlainite economic imperialism. In the end the
Party largely absorbed that doctrine which, ceasing
to be revolutionary, supplied the clichés for a whole
generation of politicians. The great pioneer never
achieved the leadership, but his truth went marching
on.

Certainly, the signs are that it is for such a role that
Enoch Powell is cast and that the chief internal problem for the Tory leadership during the next decade
will be that of containing and taming his disciples.
What kind of a man is the author of this challenge to
Tory orthodoxy? What is the precise nature of the
challenge? What are its potentialities for good and
evil? These questions may prove to be of far more
importance to the country's and the Party's future than
speculations about the succession to the leadership.

II

The Man

JOHN ENOCH POWELL was born in the Black Country on June 16th 1912. Both his parents were school-teachers, and he himself was a child of extreme intellectual precosity and phenomenal industry.

These qualities have borne fruit in a career probably of more varied distinction than that of any other contemporary British politician. Educated at King Edward's, Birmingham, one of the best of ancient English grammar school foundations, he went as an open scholar to Trinity, Cambridge, took a brilliant degree in Classics and collected a glittering array of academic awards including Cambridge's blue ribbon of classical scholarship, the Craven prize.

He has been a Fellow of Trinity, and a Professor of Greek at Sydney University in Australia (he was said to be the youngest professor in the Commonwealth at the time). During the war, he rose from the rank of private to that of Brigadier in the Royal Warwickshire Regiment and became a member of the General Staff. He was a member of the committee which laid the foundations for the reorganised defence forces in India

and Pakistan. He collaborated in the production of a
major work on strategy, *War in Three Dimensions*.

He has been joint head of a department in the
Conservative Research organisation, fought a celebrated by-election in a safe Labour seat, successfully
held Wolverhampton South-West for eighteen years,
in the process converting this largely working-class
constituency into a safe Conservative seat, refused office
in Governments three times, held two juniorMinisterial
posts, been an outstandingly successful Minister of
Health, and served in one Cabinet and two Shadow
Cabinets. He has been Vice-Chairman of the Conservative Party's 1922 Committee, Chairman of the
Party's Finance Committee in the Commons and a
contestant for the Leadership of the Conservative Party
on the first occasion on which that office was open to
election.

He has translated the *Historia* of Thucydides and
large parts of Herodotus, edited an ancient Welsh
manuscript (learning the language for the purpose),
published three books of verse in English, collaborated
in the production of a history of Britain, completed
much of a history of the House of Lords, written a book
on saving and innumerable pamphlets on political,
social and economic subjects. He was once an inter-
preter in Urdu.

It is not surprising that such a man should have
become a myth in his own life-time. What is more
remarkable is that the picture which has been built up
by innumerable newspaper articles and broadcast pro-
files should bear as close a relation to the truth as it
does. 'Vast intellect and phenomenal industry'—these

are the qualities which friends and critics alike concede, with only slight and somewhat peevish reservations on the part of the more intellectually gifted of his political colleagues. At every stage of his career, stories are bound to illustrate these qualities. Some are strictly verifiable, many others only mythical in the sense that they reveal the truth at the cost of much poetic invention.

Powell's contemporaries at King Edward's recall him as a pale youth with stooping shoulders almost wholly devoted to his books. He avoided games and his only relaxations seem to have been the clarinet and gymnastics. In this last activity he was, to the unending amazement of his schoolfellows, astonishingly proficient. It had the merit of providing healthy exercise and was not open to the charge of frivolity.

Even then Powell's manner was strikingly austere, though not so austere as it became when he went up to Cambridge. The only evidence of a boyish diversion which I have been able to trace is a story which itself reveals the rather primitive sense of humour which is often to be observed in ageing dons: it was, it is said, his delight to lean out of the carriage window as his school train left the station in an effort to knock the porters' hats off.

For the rest, life consisted mainly of Greek translations, performed with a precision and a literary skill which embarrassed many of his masters, and often done voluntarily for hours on end at home and with the constant encouragement of his accomplished mother.

Powell seems to have inspired awe but remarkably

little hostility in his schoolmates. They included many who have since achieved outstanding distinction, but even they seem to remember him over the years with a touch of trepidation. They find his public demeanour now almost incredibly human. Nothing, however, has surprised them more than their old school-fellow's brilliant military career. At school, Powell never joined the Officers' Training Corps and is said to have held schoolboy soldiering in undisguised contempt.

A good measure of the kind of impression he produced and the obstinacy with which it has lingered is supplied by the recollections of a man who was somewhat senior to him at King Edward's and who is now a distinguished scholar and churchman.

He remembers Powell as one of the youngest but quite the cleverest members of the classical Sixth. He also remembers feeling obliged, as secretary of the King Edward's Old Boys' Association at Cambridge, to visit the prodigy on his arrival at Trinity. He found him, on a bitter November morning, in an attic room in New Court. There was no fire in the grate and Powell, covered in an overcoat and rugs, was reading Thucydides. His visitor asked him if he would care to come to tea; Powell simply replied 'No'. In a renewed effort to break the ice, his school friend sauntered across the room and lit a cigarette. 'Please don't smoke,' said Powell.

This was the last time the two men exchanged words for getting on for twenty years. The next occasion was a visit by Powell to a university where the distinguished churchman now held an eminent post. Powell, however, was unable to recall their former acquaintance. When reminded of it, he chatted affably and had almost dissipated his host's sense of awe when, learning that he was now a standing authority on an obscure aspect of Biblical scholarship, he asked him whether he had ever read an unusually obscure work on that subject by a Levantine scholar. With a chagrin from which he has never recovered, the churchman was forced to confess that he had never heard of it. Powell himself knew it intimately.

There can be no doubt that at this stage Powell's imagination was fired by the current idea of what the true classical scholar was like, an idea founded chiefly on the personalities of Bentley and Housman. Its chief ingredients were industry, detachment and terseness— the uncharitable would say positive rudeness—in the conduct of personal relations. Powell seems to have done his best to live up to this image. His ambition was to be the greatest living authority on Thucydides and few of his contemporaries doubted that he would achieve it. Few of them either would have entertained for a moment the thought that this dedicated scholar might one day make an impact on public affairs.

The first year undergraduate who could respond to a dinner invitation from the Master of his college with the perfectly unaffected answer that he was too busy to come gave little evidence of the insinuating charm which is usually thought essential to a political career.

As with many other men, it was the war which changed the course of Powell's life. It confronted him for the first time with the need to apply his formidable intellect and his astonishing memory to practical

D

problems of organisation. It was not long before he had brilliantly vindicated the proposition that a classical education is a training for most things. His part in the organising of supply lines in the Middle East won golden opinions, but it was his transfer to India which made the decisive difference.

Powell was not the first Englishman to have his attitude towards politics and life completely revolutionised by the spectacle of the Indian Empire at work. He saw in it a unique example of the power of a minority united by a strong national tradition and equipped with the hereditary skills of a ruling class, to produce a deep and beneficent influence on a distant and alien land. He was fascinated by the extent to which British customs and British ways of thought had penetrated to the very roots of Indian life. He was fascinated by the love-hate relationship which seemed to bind rulers and ruled inextricably together. The vision of the Indian Empire appealed as much to his reason as to his romanticism; it was a unique example of the potentialities of the political art; it gave a hint of what a man might accomplish by devoting himself to the manipulation of public power.

When an account comes to be given of the evolution of Powell's political ideas, the full extent of the impact of his Indian experience will be clear. It explains the highly distinctive character of his Toryism. Paradoxically, it also explains the strong anti-imperialistic flavour of his current thinking about defence and foreign policy. The premise of Powellism is quite simply that the Indian Empire has been lost.

Meantime, his whole personality was being modified by the experience of military service. It is impossible to be a recluse in the army. It was equally impossible, however, for Powell to develop overnight into a genial messmate. His attitude towards his brother officers is well illustrated by a story which he is himself fond of telling.

He once had to spend several days crossing the desert in a three-ton truck in the company of a typical cavalry officer—a characteristic product of the public school system and a man of fairly exalted social rank, but of only modest academic attainments. Powell put the occasion, he says, to the best possible use by giving his companion a concise course of instruction in Greek and Roman history in return for a detailed description of the appurtenances of an English gentleman.

Both felt themselves to have benefited immensely from the exchange. In particular, it gave Powell his introduction to the theoretical principles of fox-hunting. On his return to England, he soon joined a hunt, travelling to its meets on the tube.

Powell is almost entirely destitute of social self-consciousness and is wholly free from anything which might be stigmatised as snobbery. He has, however, a detached and almost scientific interest in the traditions and customs of what used to be called the English ruling class. The romantic elements in his philosophy of politics still consist largely of admiration for the techniques of social and political leadership which that class evolved, and which found their fullest expression in the Government of the old Empire.

No doubt, the fact that Powell was ready to engage in this purposeful conversation represented a striking advance towards gregariousness. As an undergraduate and a young don, he would, report suggests, have regarded even this exercise as lamentably trivial.

The humanisation of Powell, however, was a long process, and the most important factor in it was undoubtedly his marriage in 1952 to Pamela Wilson, once his secretary at the Conservative Research Department and a soldier's daughter. Innumerable stories are told of their courtship which did not run smooth. There was the initial difficulty that Powell seldom if ever addressed his secretary for any other purpose than to give her an instruction. She is alleged to have taken bets with her colleagues on how long it would be before she could induce him to bid her good morning.

When marriage came, however, it produced an instant and dramatic effect on Powell's character, an effect far more marked than it does upon the characters of most men. His austerity diminished; his essentially friendly nature became more obvious even to casual acquaintances; he ceased to be a total abstainer from alcohol and graduated via an occasional glass of sherry to an appreciation of wines. He was said by those who knew him well to be 'greatly relaxed'. He has remained a far more domestic animal than most politicians. Much of his work is done from home, his wife still often acting as his secretary. He is a conspicuously devoted father of two daughters.

In short, his domestic surroundings and household arrangements are precisely those in which any politician in a twentieth-century democracy would wish to be imagined by his constituents. In Powell's case, the effect is genuine.

At a deeper level, it may be supposed that the development of Powell's personality since before the war has been influenced by his conversion to the Anglican faith. He is a punctilious churchman. As a young man he was a confirmed atheist. His moral convictions were humanist and Hellenic. He was also considerably affected by his reading of Nietzsche. His critics have been delighted to discover these lines in a poem which he published in the '30s:

> I hate the ugly, hate the old,
> I hate the lame and weak.
> But most of all I hate the dead,
> Who lie so still in their earthen bed,
> And never dare to rise.

Many a young man who has afterwards progressed to unchallenged respectability has written as wildly and as culpably before. Yet, it would be idle to maintain that these lines convey no clue to the character of Powell. He still believes in the inevitability of conflict between nations and men and, in certain fields, in the positive fruitfulness of such conflict. His Christianity, it need hardly be said, is not of the soft or sentimental kind. His perfectionism is now tempered by a belief in original sin, his rationality by adoption of universal compassion.

The final result of all this is a character strikingly different from the conventional idea of what a politician is like. Powell, it is true, no longer gives the impression which he made so powerfully on his Cambridge contemporaries of being simply 'bloody-

minded'. Yet, he is almost wholly destitute of smooth-
ness. It is not only his carefully prepared political
speeches which are rigorously classical in structure and
remorselessly precise in expression. Even his casual
conversation has these qualities. It is still intensely
unnerving to those who meet him for the first time.
They find their fumbling questions taken literally,
analysed and converted into rational statements of
what they 'meant to say'. They receive lucid but elaborate answers in rhythmic periods consisting largely of
subordinate clauses. Oddly enough, the impression is
not that of a man who is 'showing off' his intellectual
brilliance, but rather of one who has no choice but to
exercise it. His audience also gets strongly the impression of a man who has already made up his
mind.

Powell seldom talks for the purpose of clarifying
his own thoughts. They have already been thoroughly
formulated and documented long before they are expressed. They are usually maintained with an obstinacy
which is sometimes hard to distinguish from fanaticism.
The intellectual wrapping in which they are presented
is often so impressive that the flaws in the argument
only become clear, to the infinite frustration of his
adversaries, long after the argument is over. 'Powell,'
one of his former Cabinet colleagues remarked, 'has
the best mind in politics until it has been made up.'

What is most perturbing, however, is Powell's habit
of applying the same methods to the discussion of
everything, however trivial. He will discuss the best
method of mending a sliding-door cupboard (he is a
competent carpenter) with the same display of system

and erudition as he applies to describing the functions
of the small investor or interpreting a small incident in
the Wars of the Roses. It is a surprising tribute to
the quality of the performance that even his worst
enemies have never called him a bore.

From the point of view of this study, two mutually
inconsistent views of Powell's character remain to be
explained. In the first place, there is the impression,
which is certainly his greatest political asset, that he
is a man of 'extraordinary integrity'. The 'integrity' of
Enoch Powell has been a constant subject of comment
from the Press for many years. The quality is not easy
to define which explains, no doubt, the frequency with
which it is attributed. Like most other men in public
life, Powell is unswervingly honest in the conduct of
personal relations. This is so much the rule, however,
that only the exceptions to it are worthy of special note.
What has been claimed for Powell is that, in the
conduct of political life, he consults only his principles
and that no consideration of mere expediency will
divert him from the duty of stating and supporting
them to the best of his ability.

Insofar as this implies that Powell is indifferent to
the consequences of his political actions, that he is, so
to speak, 'a monk in politics', it is an almost fantastically false view. Few men calculate more closely the
effects of their words and actions. Insofar as it means
simply that Powell considers deeply the moral implications of what he is doing, it is undoubtedly right.

While being praised by the Press for his integrity,
however, Powell has more than once been accused by
his colleagues of showing less than total loyalty. Many

of those who have worked closely with him have
carried away the view that his actions are unpredict-
able. The most recent and outstanding example of that
view was the reaction of his Shadow Cabinet colleagues
to his speech on immigration. Nevertheless, there have
been precedents: more than once those who have sat
in intimate conclave with him have been surprised by
what he has later said in public about the subjects on
which they were deliberating.

How are these apparently opposite reputations to be
reconciled? The key, I believe, is to be found in the
solitariness which even now is one of Powell's most
outstanding characteristics. The army, marriage, reli-
gion and politics have transformed Powell's personality
beyond instant recognition, but they have not destroyed
his ultimate detachment. His colleagues say that in
Cabinet and in Committee he talks comparatively little.
When he does it is to announce and defend with precision conclusions at which he has already arrived in
private. Most men's minds are formed in conversation
with their peers; Powell's is not.

Much that passes for loyalty and comradeship in
politics depends on the observance of a convention
of relaxed and even slovenly conversation. Men win
trust by seeming to have nothing to conceal and by
conducting their thinking in public. The very qualities
which make Powell an awkward colleague also unfit
him for conspiracy. What is more, his unsparing
intellectual honesty leads him, both in public and private relations, to a more systematic, carefully thought-
out definition of his moral obligations than most men
are capable of. It is the very rigour and exactness of

that definition which often arouses the suspicion of those who work with him.

He is, as a consequence, never wholly absorbed in a team; his relations with others are systematised on the basis of a precise casuistry from which he never deviates. He knows, to his own satisfaction, exactly what candour requires him to reveal to his colleagues and what he is justified in keeping to himself. Inevitably, his own ideas on this point sometimes prove different from theirs. On these occasions, he is often genuinely surprised and injured by the ferocity of their reactions. Yet, the impact of the shock, one suspects, is generally reduced by Powell's lack, rare in a politician, of any conspicuous wish to please. Generous, affectionate and almost imperturbably (one might say complacently) tolerant by nature, Powell's loyalty is, nevertheless, primarily to principles. Men with far less exacting consciences and infinitely slovenly minds have a larger capacity for political friendship.

This temperamental isolation, and the strength and weaknesses which go with it may well prove in the end to be the decisive factors in Powell's political fate.

III

The Man in Politics

POWELL entered the House of Commons in 1950 as a distinguished member of the Butler kindergarten. He had worked in the Conservative Research Department. He was of comparatively humble origin. His war record was outstanding.

In all these respects, he was typical of a group of young men who, it was thought, were designed to propel the Conservative Party into the twentieth century. They would re-interpret Conservative principles. They would put an end to the notion that the Conservative Party was an upper-class institution controlled by the stupid. They would provide an intellectually valid answer to Socialism.

In the eyes of the public, they were progressives—men who had liberated themselves from ancient prejudices and would shortly liberate their party as well. They were representatives of the Disraelian tradition. They would prove that there was a policy of reform which was distinct from Socialism but nonetheless radical in its content.

The 'One Nation' group which some of these young

men and others of like kind in the '50 entry formed, published a series of pamphlets which sketched the outlines
of this new Conservatism. They argued in favour of a
more discriminatory application of the now vast resources of public money spent on welfare. They pointed
out the limitations of the system of flat-rate contributions and flat-rate benefits which followed from the
acceptance of the Beveridge Report.

They emphasised that compulsory insurance was
itself merely another form of taxation and that it had
in any case proved inadequate to raise the vast revenues
now needed to sustain the social services. Wherever it
had to be supplemented out of the proceeds of direct
taxation, there was an overwhelming case for distributing the resulting funds to those who needed them most
rather than spreading them over the whole community.
There was nothing intrinsically immoral, they contended, about the principle of the means test.

All these suggestions were made, however, against
the background of an assumed programme of generous
and constantly expanding welfare. It occurred to no
one to suppose that these Young Conservatives were
recommending a return to the Poor Law or stood anywhere else than in the vanguard of enlightened social
thinking. Their doctrine was that it was the business of
the State to establish a generous minimum standard of
welfare below which no citizen would be permitted to
fall. They were the pioneers of that principle of
'selectivity' which is now so fashionable among politicians of both Left and Right.

Equally, their views of the economy were liberal and
moderate. They believed in capitalism and competition

and wished to free the Conservative Party from the kind of restrictive economic policies which it had pursued in the '30s. Nevertheless, capitalism and competition were only the premises of their argument. They expressly reserved to the State the right not only to intervene by fiscal means to control the pace at which the economy moved, but also, when necessary, to use such methods as direct import controls to achieve results which free economic activity could not. They had no doubts about its being one of the functions of government to provide for a high and stable level of employment. Here again, they were essentially 'middle of the road' men.

Powell's own contribution to this restatement of the principles of social and economic Conservatism was recognised as outstanding. Yet he remained intensely preoccupied with imperial affairs and in particular with the destinies of India. It is said that while he was working for the Conservative Research Department in the years before he entered Parliament he was sent to see Winston Churchill to assist in the preparation of a speech on India. When the interview was over, Churchill rang up the Research Department to ask, 'Who is that young madman who has been telling me how many divisions I would need to re-conquer India?'

Powell bitterly opposed the decision to set a date for the ending of British rule before agreement had been reached on what was to follow it.

He passionately believed in the duty and the possibility of preserving the Indian Empire until eventually it had evolved into a stable and self-governing part of the Commonwealth. The abandonment of India seemed to him to be as much an act of self-mutilation as the abandonment of Kent might have seemed to others.

In the House of Commons, Powell was one of the original members of the Suez group and as such voted against the Anglo-Egyptian agreement which provided for the phased withdrawal of British troops from the canal zone. In short, at this stage of his career, Powell was a liberal imperialist, committed wholeheartedly to the view that Britain had a world role.

What has to be explained is the almost incredible contrast between Powell in the early 1950s and Powell today. In home policy, the moderate Butlerite, the defender of a tempered form of capitalism, has become the apparently fanatical advocate of a laissez-faire economy in which the State is limited to the function of an overall monetary regulator and a keeper of the general rules. In foreign affairs he is now, at least by reputation, the ruthless advocate of a policy of withdrawal from distant overseas commitments and total concentration on the defence of Europe.

This transformation would be staggering enough in anyone. In Powell's case, it has to be reconciled with a reputation for unsparing intellectual consistency and total contempt for political expediency. What becomes of the iron man of principle and the political ascetic with his eyes firmly fixed on the eternal verities? Would it not be as easy to make out a case for the proposition that Powell is the most flexible of politicians, a man given not only to altering his conclusions but frequently to revising his premises?

A glance at some of the highlights of Powell's career

in the past eighteen years will help, I believe, to explain the paradox.

Oddly but characteristically one of the ablest and most profoundly moving speeches of Powell's early political career was delivered in the House of Commons on March 3rd, 1953, on the second reading of the Royal Titles Bill. The measure provided for certain changes in the styles and titles of Her Majesty the Queen and embodied the agreements reached at a Commonwealth Prime Ministers' Conference in the previous year.

To most people it undoubtedly appeared to be a matter primarily of technical and legal interest. It gave formal expression to the theory which had been slowly developing over the years that the Queen was to be regarded as lawful sovereign of a number of separate and independent states, but she might properly be described, for example, as 'Queen of Australia' and 'Queen of Canada'. It also instituted a completely new title, 'Head of the Commonwealth', designed to permit the accommodation within the Commonwealth of countries like India which had elected to become Republics. It omitted the adjective 'British' before the word 'Commonwealth'.

In all these respects Powell found the Bill intensely and fundamentally objectionable. Defying his Party whip, he voted against it.

His speech was at once closely reasoned and passionate.

The term 'Realms', he declared, 'which is to appear in the new title, is an emphatic statement that Her Majesty is the Queen of a considerable number of kingdoms. Hitherto, that has not been this country's acceptance of the term'. This new concept, he contended, destroyed the nature of the British Empire and Commonwealth as a unit bound together by common loyalty to a person. It transformed it into a fortuitous aggregation of independent communities. The omission of the word 'British' was a gratuitous repudiation of history. The idea of a Head of the Commonwealth to whom allegiance, in the strict meaning of the word, was not owed was an absurdity. To describe the Queen as Queen of the United Kingdom and 'Her Other Realms and Territories' was strictly meaningless. 'We describe a Monarch by designating the territory of which he is a Monarch. To say that he is Monarch of a certain territory and his other realms and territories is as good as to say that he is king of his kingdom. We have perpetuated a solecism in the title we are proposing to attach to our Sovereign.'

It would be easy to dismiss these scruples as pedantic. Plainly, however, Powell believed that they carried decisive political significance. That significance he describes in another passage: 'It is this instinctive recognition of being parts of a whole, which means that in certain circumstances individual, local, partial interests would be sacrified to the general interest, that constitutes unity. Unless there is some such instinctive deliberate determination, there is no unity. There may be alliance, indeed. We may have alliance between two Sovereign Powers for the pursuit of common interest for a particular or for an undefined period; but that is not unity. That is not the maintenance or the creation of any such entity as we refer to by the name "Empire" or "Commonwealth".'

In retrospect, it seems that the Royal Titles Bill represented a decisive turning point in Powell's career. It gave formal recognition to the end of the British Empire and indeed to the end of the British Commonwealth of Nations in any sense in which that phrase could be intelligible to him. To others it seemed that it merely gave formal recognition to blatant facts— the dissolution of the Indian Empire, the admission of republics to the Commonwealth, the birth of a new state of affairs in which it was only too easy to envisage the possibility of member states of the Commonwealth taking up arms against each other.

To most Conservatives it appeared that the Commonwealth had for a long time been a wholly indefinable institution, that the Statute of Westminster with its talk about autonomy and equality itself postulated an institution which defied juridical classification. They felt, however, that the accidents of a common history had created certain common sentiments which it might be politically valuable to preserve at the cost of juridical confusion and logical inconsistency. If a number of far-flung countries were drawn into more or less habitual co-operation with each other by an indistinct combination of material interest and historic sentiment, might there not be merits in maintaining that co-operation for as long as possible? If certain vague, high-sounding, ultimately indefensible phrases might be found to contribute to that end, what was the objection to employing them on solemn state occasions?

Already, as Powell knew, a mortal blow had been struck at the old conception of the Commonwealth by the British Nationality Act of 1948 which made citizen-

ship of the Commonwealth derivative from citizenship
of one of its member states instead of natural allegiance
to the Crown. From within the Research Department
at the time he had argued might and main but vainly
to persuade the Tory Party to oppose it. The Royal
Titles Bill merely took the inevitable process a stage
further.

No doubt Powell's horror at the measure owed
something to his romanticism, but it also owed much
to his political realism. Gradually and painfully he was
being forced to accommodate himself to a world in
which the British Empire did not exist. The premise
of his thinking had so far been that the first duty, the
elementary *raison d'être*, of the British Government was
the defence of that Empire. It was not open to a British
statesman to ask whether, in terms of the happiness
and prosperity of the people of the United Kingdom
that Empire was worth defending. It was not open to
him to consider whether other alliances offered greater
security at less cost. The Empire and the Commonwealth were not, in Powell's eyes, an alliance. They
constituted a unit the parts of which, including the
United Kingdom, might at any moment be asked to
sacrifice themselves to the whole. Once that unit had
ceased to exist the premises of Powell's thinking about
politics had to be revolutionised. That process, no
doubt, was already well under way; the end of British
rule in India had started it off.

It was merely characteristic of Powell's thought that
the theoretical recognition of the new facts in the Royal
Titles Bill should have seemed to him to be of such
decisive importance. We had not only ceased to be

an Empire, we had even abandoned the attempt to convince ourselves that we were one. The intellectual confusions in which we had thus become involved were not merely intrinsically repulsive, they would in fact have the effect of putting our policy in shackles by making us behave as though we had power which in fact we lacked and obligations which in fact we had discarded. One of Powell's distinctive convictions is that it is impossible to go on behaving sensibly while constantly talking nonsense.

From 1953 onwards, Powell slowly and painfully abandoned his imperialism. His connection with the Suez group ended shortly after the signing of the Anglo-Egyptian treaty. He was not among those who felt conspicuous enthusiasm, for instance, for the belated attempt to reassert British power in the Middle East in 1956. Once vital positions had been abandoned, it was idle to lust after their recovery. It is easy to see and indeed to trace the steps by which Powell has progressed to his present position over defence and foreign policy. He is now disposed to argue that the British Empire always cost the people of these islands more than it was worth. It was a burden to be borne from duty. Freed from it, we are at liberty to rethink our defence and foreign policies starting from the assumption that their aim is simply the defence of these islands.

This transition in Powell's thinking is characteristic of his mind. It supplies the key not only to his current programme but also to his whole method of thought. In academic language, Powell can be correctly classified as a historical empiricist. He is not, that is to say, a man who starts out from abstract principles which he proceeds to apply to changing situations. Equally, however, he is not an empiricist in the sense in which that expression is used by such political commentators as have heard of it. He does not, that is to say, believe that politics is a hand-to-mouth affair, a succession of expedients to meet unforeseen and unforeseeable situations, a series of cases each of which must be judged on its own merits. In his mind, circumstances are almost everything not only because they limit the possibilities of action but also because they positively indicate the kind of action required. There is something of Bismarckian mysticism in his conviction that history is intimating to us where we should go and how we should get there.

To him any given set of historical facts points to a policy. There is a latent order in human affairs which it is the business of statesmanship to perceive and realise. This is, of course, not a form of determinism. Powell suspects and denounces more strongly than any other contemporary politician the argument of inevitability, the habit of recommending unwelcome policies on the assumption that they are going to happen anyway. He regards this as the most insidious and one of the most despicable weapons of Socialist propaganda.

Politicians, he believes, are always free to ignore the intimations of history, but they do so at their own and at their nation's peril. It is open to them to behave as though they are ruling an empire when they are not. It is open to them to assume that they are governing a country which is strong enough to establish and control its own markets by adding political to economic power, when in fact they are presiding over a relatively weak and overcrowded little island which can exist only by selling its wares in a highly competitive international market. Disaster is the penalty for such errors.

To accept all this, however, does not imply an attitude of political quietism, of philosophic resignation in face of overwhelming forces. There is nothing that Powell despises more vigorously than such an attitude. His romanticism prevents him from even entertaining the idea that Britain may not have a great and glorious destiny. The problem is merely to discover what kind of destiny that is, what sort of a nation history is bidding her become.

Powell has solved that problem to his own intellectual satisfaction. The starting-point of his political thinking is that Britain must in future regard herself as a European power. It is on the Continent of Europe alone—or almost alone—that she can effectively apply force. By concentrating all the force she has there, she can maximise her influence in the world. Hence, the total reversal of Powell's position in this field—a reversal of which he is perfectly conscious and which he reasonably defends as intellectually consistent.

Hence also, the striking difference between the tone of Powell's utterances on this subject and that of other politicians who, without his philosophy of history, have also drawn the obvious conclusion that commitments East of Suez are no longer practicable for Britain. To them this is the counsel of prudence and restraint. To Powell it is a summons to a new kind of national mission as capable of eliciting heroic qualities and stimulating patriotic pride as was the mission of empire.

Doubts must remain, of course, about the extent to which this difference is real and not merely a further example of Powell's skill as an orator. There are those who contend that in his approach to foreign and defence policy Powell is merely using the signal to advance in order to convey a command to retreat. The justice of this accusation must be analysed later. Even if it were accepted, however, the achievement would remain remarkable and would not be destitute of political significance. National self-confidence is an important element in the effectiveness of any foreign policy. To preserve and increase it while inducing a nation to acknowledge its limitations realistically is itself a quite considerable feat.

Doubts must also remain, of course, about the realism of Powell's thought on this subject. Like the rest of his doctrines, his philosophy of defence is distinguished by almost fanatical rigour. Here as elsewhere, one gets the impression that Powell attributes somewhat too much certitude and precision to the intimations of history. He seems sometimes to assume that there are pre-ordained, neatly distinguished categories into which nations must perforce fit themselves—imperial power (far flung commitments, tradition of hierarchic government, economic policy tending mildly towards dirigism) or small island on verge of potentially hostile continent (must live by wit and competitive power of individuals in trade). Is a nation's role ever precisely as clear as this?

Powell is of course fully conscious of the fact that the foundations of British foreign policy cannot be transformed overnight. He has found it compatible

with his conscience and with the extravagant importance which he attaches to verbal consistency to be the
defence spokesman of a party which preponderantly
rejects his own fundamental views, which treasures
imperialism not only as a memory but also as an essential ingredient, in however modernised guise it may
appear in its philosophy of politics.

He was acutely conscious of the truth of Burke's
maxim that duties are the preachers of circumstance.
An imperial power in decline of necessity finds itself
saddled with commitments which it cannot honourably
drop at a moment's notice. It cannot relieve itself of the
responsibility for the consequences which will follow
on its withdrawals of power. It must show elementary
loyalty to its friends by at least giving them adequate
notice of the intention to desert them. The proper
timing of these strategic retreats will for long remain
one of the crucial problems of British policy.

In a sense, however, it is hard to imagine how Powell
would have survived politically during the last few
years without the aid of this problem. It enabled him
to join with other Conservatives in the downright
condemnation of strategic decisions by the Government of the ultimate necessity of which he is profoundly
convinced. The blessed epithet 'premature' has more
than once come to his aid. This, plus his passionate
advocacy of adequate preparedness for a Continental
European war, has given him an indispensable reputation among his political supporters for militancy. It
has enabled him simultaneously and in judicious instal-
ments to attempt the re-education of his own party while
appearing to defend its largely out-of-date positions.

There have been few more engagingly ironic spectacles in British politics recently than the bewildered reactions of traditionally minded right-wing sections of Tory opinion to the mental gymnastics of their former Shadow Minister of Defence. The Monday Club honours him as a right-wing extremist, only to discover, or at least partially to apprehend, when it invites him to dinner that he is the strenuous advocate of East of Suez policies which they have so far regarded as the prerogative of the Socialist left. The apparent discrepancies are easily recognisable but not so easily accepted to minds less complex and sophisticated than Powell's.

Here then emerge three essential characteristics of Powell's thought and action, characteristics which can repeatedly be observed. The first is his conviction, amounting to faith, that political principles are to be arrived at by studying the facts of history and contemporary life. The second is a tendency to deduce from these facts rigidly coherent policies. The inevitable consequence of this rigour is that when Powell's mind, in response to the facts, changes, it changes more dramatically than anyone else's.

The third is a willingness, seldom combined with even half Powell's capacity for clear thinking, to bow in practice to the necessity of politics—having defined his ideal to recognise that it can be only gradually approached and partially achieved. Hence it is that the descriptions romantic, realist, intellectual and shrewd politician can all be applied to him with some show of fairness.

What remains to be explained is the emergence of Powell, once a fairly moderate Butlerite, as the exponent of an extreme doctrine of governmental non-intervention in economic affairs. In this respect, his resignation from the post of financial secretary to the Treasury in January 1958 is another decisive and illuminating moment. He resigned with the Chancellor, Peter Thorneycroft, and with his colleague, Nigel Birch, the economic secretary to the Treasury.

His decision was regarded at the time by many Conservatives both as an act of grievous disloyalty to his party and as a form of political suicide. Powell's reputation was far from being well established. The financial secretaryship to the Treasury is a well-worn stepping stone to Cabinet rank. It was more than averagely audacious of him to flout his superiors after an extremely short period of office.

What is more, the Conservative Party was at the time in an extremely poor state. It had not yet recovered from the trauma of Suez, and the authority of its leader Harold Macmillan was far from being firmly established. The simultaneous resignation of three Treasury Ministers at such a time was predicted by many to be a mortal blow. Comparatively few Conservatives shared the imperturbable complacency of the Prime Minister who, in a phrase which later became famous, dismissed the whole incident as an example of 'little local difficulties'.

The resignation issue was extremely narrowly defined and as such, some people said, particularly calculated to appeal to Powell's literal mind. The three Ministers resigned because the financial estimates for the ensuing year provided for an increase in public expenditure whereas the Government was committed to keeping its own expenditure at the existing level. Competent arithmeticians calculated that the difference between the Treasury Ministers and their colleagues amounted to the sum of £50,000,000.

Nevertheless, there had been a departure from stated intention. The Ministers concerned argued that this was all the graver because private industry had been repeatedly appealed to to keep its own expenditure stable. This appeal, in their view, implied a bargain which the Government was under a moral obligation to observe in planning its own activity during the ensuing year.

Looking back on this resignation, Powell has been heard to say three things. He has been in the habit of insisting that it was an event 'sufficient unto itself', by which he presumably means that it was a response to certain immediate obligations of conscience in a particular situation and not a general comment on the whole trend of the Macmillan Government's policy. He has also emphasised the duty which a junior Minister must feel to a superior who has been let down by his Cabinet colleagues. And he has also insisted that the decision to resign, though naturally discussed between themselves, was taken independently by all three of the men concerned.

In retrospect, it seems probable that the occasion had a far larger significance than this interpretation suggests. Certainly, the consideration of loyalty bulked large in Powell's mind. He refused to serve under Macmillan until Thorneycroft had also been re-

admitted to the Government. As later events have
shown, Powell's view of what he owes to his colleagues
may differ from theirs, but his conduct on this occasion
and in the months that followed shows clearly the
strength of his devotion to his own code. Powell must
have been aware, however, that far larger issues than
those of personal allegiance were involved in this
dangerous and dramatic decision.

Fifty million pounds, it is true, is a small enough
sum—though, as a matter of fact, Powell asserted
publicly at the time that the sum in question was substantially larger. To the mature political mind of R. A.
Butler, the resignations seemed for that reason to be
an almost incredible act of pedantry, but one not at
all incompatible with the view which he had formed
of the personality of Powell who had long since ceased
to be his protégé. By resigning, however, Powell had
taken a step on what was in future to become his fundamental conviction about economic policy—that the
main size and function of government expenditure is
the crucial factor in inflation and in economic progress.

Thorneycroft's successor at the Exchequer—the
judicious, humane, unambitious Heathcote Amory—
certainly did not inaugurate an era of profligacy. In
essence he seemed to be maintaining the same tough
fiscal policy as Thorneycroft. Yet, looking back, it is
at least arguable that these resignations constituted a
turning-point in the economic policy of the Macmillan
government. Financial stringency, at least by comparison with former governments, remained the rule. Under
Selwyn Lloyd, it was to take the extreme form of a
wages freeze. Yet public expenditure continued to

increase and the number of civil servants continued to expand.

In 1958, the Macmillan government had shrunk from the task of making the combating of inflation by strict monetary policies its main aim. It had decided to put the maintenance of expanding programmes of welfare first. Inevitably, it was driven to put the main burden of restraint on the private sector. Inevitably also, it was driven to look for other than fiscal methods of stemming the declining value of money. The era of the National Incomes Commission and the National Economic Development Council was at hand.

The last years of Macmillan's premiership introduced a modified version of socialist economic policy with all the characteristics which Powell has since so vehemently denounced—increasing public expenditure and the attempt to offset it by various forms of direct economic control—less effective but no less offensive in Powell's eyes, for resting mainly on appeals to voluntary co-operation rather than commands with the force of law.

Powell now plainly thinks that an important part of his mission in politics is to challenge and destroy the collectivist assumptions which marked the end of the Macmillan era. By resigning in 1958 he laid on record publicly and emphatically the standards by which he condemned these heresies. He may fairly claim to have made his protest at the beginning of the descent. Another plank in the Powellite platform was thus firmly laid.

But there is yet another paradox to be explained. Having thus made his protest against the trends of government policy, Powell rejoined the Macmillan administration in July 1960. He bore his share of the collective responsibility for the conduct of that administration until it ended in October 1963. During the last fifteen months of this period, he bore the larger share of that responsibility which belongs to members of the Cabinet as distinct from junior Ministers. Throughout the entire three years, he was Minister of Health and as such answerable for a vast and absolutely, though not relatively, growing element in public expenditure.

If the Macmillan Government had erred on the side of profligacy to the tune of £50 million in 1958, it erred far more grievously afterwards. What is more, all those other features in economic policy which Powell is particularly inclined to condemn—planning on the basis of voluntary co-operation between Government and industry, attempts to control wages and other incomes by enlisting the force of public opinion behind the judgment of official bodies and so on—became increasingly pronounced.

By the time Macmillan retired, Incomes Policy had indeed achieved the status of a *deus ex machina*. It was to be the method by which the Government would be able to prevent inflation while maintaining perpetual economic expansion and constantly increasing public expenditure on the provision of communal services. It is, of course, no new or discreditable thing for a Minister to belong to a Government the policies of which he does not wholly approve. But for the convention which authorises such behaviour, indeed, Cabinet Government would be impossible. It is for the individual conscience to decide which compromises are acceptable and which are not. Yet, the gulf between Powell and his colleagues at this time seems in retrospect to have been wide enough to raise the question of whether he should have remained in office.

At the Ministry of Health, he threw himself with unbounded zeal into the running of a vast, monolithic institution. He did not have to be goaded into making ambitious plans for its development. His ten-year schemes for hospital building and for the development of the Health and Welfare Service were unprecedented exercises in official forecasting. They make an astonishing contrast with the view now expressed almost daily by Powell that it is presumptuous for a Government to try and look even a year ahead.

Powell is passionately interested in administration. Indeed, he has often reflected that, when in power, he finds it hard to confine his mind to the generalities which are the proper concern of the political head of a department. It is said that, as Financial Secretary to the Treasury, he achieved an unrivalled detailed knowledge of the tax system within three weeks. When he was at the Ministry of Health, his officials, who acquired an unusual liking and respect for him, soon lost that sense of superior knowledge which they normally feel towards their political masters. Powell's temperament drove him to administer with almost frenetic zeal.

By the same token, he was not popular with the doctors. This, no doubt, was in part due to the extravagant expectations aroused by his appointment. At last, it was felt, the Ministry of Health would be in the hands of a man who respected professional independence and had a genuine belief in consumer choice. Instead, they found themselves saddled with a rigid administrator who could never be persuaded to yield a point and whom they accused of imposing his will by such age-old administrative techniques as the production of an incessant flow of complex and misleading figures. My conversations with the more politically minded members of the medical profession (and over the years they have been numerous) give me the impression that they distrusted and disliked Powell more intensely than any other Minister of Health since Aneurin Bevan who at least had the excuse of his political affiliations.

The method by which Powell reconciled himself to his role in the Macmillan government is not hard to define. The National Health Service existed. The assumptions on which it was based—that it should be free at the point of reception and that it should be universal—were at the time politically unchallenge-able. Decades of sustained persuasion might be necessary before these assumptions could be modified. In the meantime, therefore, the task was to administer this service as efficiently as possible. It would continue to exhibit the defects of a monopoly; the plans for its development might be vitiated, indeed, certainly would be vitiated, by unforeseeable contingencies. This was no excuse for failing to make those plans. A system which depended for its efficacy on administration must be administered as energetically and as efficiently as possible. Powell has never wholly expelled from his mind the proposition that, if life is not to be controlled by the interplay of market forces, it will be better controlled by strong than by weak government. Charged with administering a socialist state, he would plan more not less than the socialists.

What he could do, what he incessantly did, during this period of power was to exhibit his scepticism of the entire system. He would have no truck with the conventional poppy-cock which had been developed to prove that the National Health Service was not only an institution with some merits but an institution with all possible merits. He delighted, for instance, in challenging the notion that the undoubted improvement in the nation's health since the war was attributable entirely or even preponderantly to a free health service. It was due primarily, he contended, to advances in medical science which were largely the result of the war.

He challenged with equal force the doctrine that expenditure on National Health necessarily increased the gross national product. Nothing could be more characteristic of his attitude at this time, for example, than his Lloyds Roberts lecture to the Royal Society of Medicine in January 1962.

How, he asked, could a necessary and inevitable relationship be assumed between public expenditure on health and national productivity? If such a relationship did exist, it would follow that if all the nation's money were spent on health the nation's productivity would reach an unprecedented zenith. Manifestly, and by definition, it would not. It must therefore be that increased public expenditure on health will fail, beyond a certain point, to enhance productivity. What is more, if the nation's spending on doctors and hospitals were to be related entirely to its economic value in terms of production the Health Service would have to be so organised as to concentrate on the needs of those who, by medical attention, could be rendered fit or more fit for work. Expenditure on prolonging economically useless lives would have to be abandoned. The whole trend of medical progress would have to be reversed. Such a ruthless regime would be morally intolerable. To reject it, however, implied admitting that there was a potential conflict between the wish for a healthier nation and the wish for greater material prosperity. Once admit this conflict, and the size of proper provision for National Health would become a possible topic of rational discussion.

Later on, Powell was to write a widely misunderstood book which argued that the National Health Service was full of defects, and that these defects arose from its very nature as a 'free service'. He did not suggest, however, that it was politically possible to challenge the concept of a free service. This undoubtedly represented his attitude while he was at the Ministry.

A characteristic example of that attitude was his response to the widespread demand (which at one time the Conservative Party had officially supported) for the extension to patients in the private medical service of the right to free prescriptions. On the face of it, the idea would have everything to commend it to an advocate of free choice in the social services. Bevan himself had accepted the principle that the whole or any part of the medical service should be freely available to all covered by the National Insurance scheme. It could be contended that those who paid for their own doctors in addition to making their compulsory subscriptions to the scheme were making a voluntary contribution to the Health Service by relieving the crushing burden on National Health doctors. Why should they be required to bear the additional burden of financing their prescriptions?

To the considerable dismay of the medical lobby in the Conservative Party Powell would have no truck at all with the extension of free prescriptions. The practical and overwhelming objection to it was that it would cost the Treasury more money which could only properly be financed by cuts in the rest of the Health programme.

His theoretical objections were more casuistical in character. Diagnosis and prescription, he contended, were different ends of the same activity, not separate branches of the Health Service. It was perfectly proper that a man who paid for the services of his own G.P. should be committed on that G.P.'s advice to have a free operation in a state hospital; the idea that he should also be committed, on the strength of a private prescription, to get a free packet of aspirins from the chemist was an intolerable affront to logic. Technically, Powell was right in the sense that no operation within the Health Service arises in theory from direct recommendation by a private doctor, but the distinction is one more easily acceptable to the mind of a doctrinaire bureaucrat than to that of most patients.

Powell equally resisted the suggestion that private patients were in any sense subsidising the public sector. The theory was that if these patients ceased to provide

F

for themselves they would perforce join the lists of National Health doctors, thereby costing the Government money.

To this, Powell replied that National Health doctors were paid out of a common pool, the size of which was determined by what the Treasury could afford; that, since the pool would remain constant, the only effect of increasing the number of National Health patients would be to reduce the capitation fee which could be provided for each of them. The effect of a mass migration of private patients into the public sector, therefore, would merely be to make National Health doctors work harder for the remuneration they already got. Q.E.D. an increase in National Health patients saves the Treasury nothing—ergo the Treasury cannot be asked to compensate, out of gratitude, those who contribute to the Health Service without using it.

The assumption of this characteristic reasoning is, of course, that the amount of money which the State spends on the provision of family doctors is a fixed quantity within limits which no likely diversion of patients from the State to the private sector would even begin to approach.

What Powell was in practice arguing, by methods peculiar to himself, was the defensible proposition that the advantages of a freer choice of doctor were not great enough to justify either the diversion of public funds from other activities than health or the diversion from other parts of the Health Service to the provision of family doctors. The issue was marginal, but it indicates the logical rigour with which Powell is capable of deducing false conclusions from wrong premises.

It is equally true, of course, that his administration was outstandingly humane. He favoured decentralisation—where possible. He believed in the importance of voluntary and philanthropic supplement to what the State provided. He showed a deep personal interest in mental health.

No Minister of Health has done more either to abate the rigour of hospital rules in such matters as visiting patients. He investigated every individual complaint sent to him with much more care than was necessary to secure a reputation for being a thoroughly humane Minister. Recognising that he had a virtual monopoly in the purchase of drugs, he sought, in the arrangements he made with the drug manufacturers, to reproduce (again as far as possible) the conditions of a free market. What he did not do was to contemplate even for a moment any fundamental change in the character of the service design either to extend private choice or to expose it to the beneficent influences of his blessed law of supply and demand. At least, in the view of many, he tended, on the contrary, to be 'an over-mighty Minister'. He was also a brilliantly efficient Minister.

Superficially, all this is highly reminiscent. It is as though Powell's thought had undergone in relation to domestic politics the same kind of transformation which it underwent in relation to foreign affairs and defence with the collapse of the Indian Empire. It is as though he had identified his departure from the Macmillan government in 1958 as a decisive moment. It is as though he reasoned that his colleagues had then taken the wrong path, that their decision was irrevocable and that the business of a statesman was to make the best of the resulting situation and to do so with zeal and logic—to see to it, in fact, that the neo-socialist society into which we were moving was as efficiently administered as was compatible with its nature.

There was of course a profound difference: Powell plainly did not believe that the effects of Macmillanite conservatism were inexpungable. Throughout his period of office he continued within the limits of Cabinet discipline to pursue the task of educating the public. He insisted on maintaining a sceptical attitude towards the institution he was running.

Powell's capacity to pursue and his taste for pursuing the two distinct roles of prophet and administrator simultaneously is undoubtedly one of the main sources of the distrust and bewilderment which he often inspires. Other politicians make compromises as drastic as his (otherwise they would be unfit for political life and would affront the specific morality on the basis of which that life is conducted). In Powell's case, the compromises are far more conscious and clearly defined than in that of most other practitioners of the trade. What is more, they have a disturbing habit of being defined or at least implied in public. This kind of conscientiousness is easily mistaken for disloyalty.

A more practical question, however, is suggested by Powell's tenure of the Ministry of Health. He administered energetically not only because he believed that the Health Service as it was constituted demanded such treatment, but also because he loved administration. How long would Powell's convinced liberalism—his passion for individual freedom and his deep scepticism of the beneficence and efficacy of government—last if he were ever effectively in charge of a government?

IV

A Turning Point

P OWELL's departure from office in 1963 presents mysteries far more profound than any which have yet been considered. Why did he refuse to serve under Sir Alec Douglas Home?

By so doing, he again incurred grave political dangers. In the course of his comparatively brief career he had already refused office twice (once from Churchill because he did not like the junior post proposed to him, once from Macmillan because he was not prepared to return to the Government without Thorneycroft) and he had also resigned once.

To add one more refusal to the list was tempting providence with a vengeance. It was tempting something more terrible than providence as well—the ire of those solid, often inarticulate elements of the Conservative Party who look for loyalty rather than devotion to principle and on whose support the success of a Conservative political career so largely depends. Powell ran this risk at a moment when the Conservative Party was in turmoil and when Tories up and down the country were hotly engaged in the familiar pursuit of urging each other not to 'rock the boat'.

Those events are still vividly imprinted on all Tory memories. During the summer the Macmillan myth had begun rapidly to disintegrate. The Government, which was increasingly unpopular, had been shaken by a gigantic personal scandal—the revelation that its Minister of War, Mr. Profumo, had deceived the House of Commons in a personal statement in order to conceal his immoral association with a young woman who was shortly to become one of the central figures in a national drama about vice and corruption in high places. Inevitably, the affair swelled to fantastic proportions. Wild accusations were made or implied against half the political establishment. Few Ministers escaped the damaging effects of the gossip. A judge's enquiry was required to investigate the whole matter before the reputation of the Cabinet for chaste and clean living could be finally vindicated.

In all this, Powell played a part the prominence of which was almost wholly accidental. Correctly, he held that the only issue of the least political importance was whether Macmillan had or had not colluded in the deception of the House. It was this deception, and not the revelations concerning Profumo's aberrations from chastity, which had inevitably brought that unfortunate politician to ruin. What was at stake was the breach of a specific and sacred rule of constitutional morality—that, in making a personal statement to the House, privileged in that it is exempted from cross-examination, a Minister of the Crown must not lie. Had it been proved that, in order to preserve his administration from scandal, Macmillan had conspired to such a lie, he would undoubtedly have had to resign.

Powell had the deepest anxieties on this point. He was not, at the outset, satisfied that the innocence of the Prime Minister was self-evident. He insisted on the closest examination of the evidence. A still unexplained leak from a Cabinet meeting produced newspaper reports to the effect that Powell and a number of other Ministers were about to resign since they could not satisfy themselves of the correctness of the Prime Minister's behaviour.

In fact, by the time this report appeared, Powell and his doubting colleagues had already become completely convinced that Macmillan had absolutely no part in any kind of attempt to mislead the Commons. After consulting with the Cabinet office, Powell resolved to make a public statement to this effect but, on their advice, refrained from doing so for a few days when a speech in the country would provide the natural occasion for such a declaration. One of the unsolicited consequences of this train of events was that the entire country waited for some time in suspense for Powell's judgment on his leader. He was already known to be a man of exacting conscience—some said a puritanical conscience—who would have no truck with lechery and lying. His positive affirmation that Macmillan had not erred was a powerful reinforcement to the Prime Minister in his distress. It helped greatly to ensure for him a majority in the Commons adequate to weather the storm.

The Profumo affair, however, had taken the lid off a great deal of mounting Tory resentment against

Macmillan. His virtue might be unassailable, but his competence and in particular the closeness of his connection with his own backbenchers was not. A sudden illness involving a need for surgery made his departure and the choice of a successor inevitable.

Several differing versions exist of what then ensued, but the essentials are not in dispute. R. A. Butler was the heir presumptive, if not the heir apparent. He was left in charge of the Government during Macmillan's illness, an unenviable lot which had fallen to him on at least two former occasions. Many had confidently expected him to succeed Eden and held, though without much evidence to support them, that even then he had been the victim of a plot. In 1962, Macmillan had appeared at last to recognise the strength of Butler's title to be next in the line of succession by making him virtually Deputy Prime Minister, a concession which he had always refused in the past. None of Butler's colleagues could rival him in the length and variety of his political experience. His services in the revitalising of the Conservative Party after 1945 were universally acknowledged.

It was known, however, that there had almost throughout the whole duration of their political careers been a strong mutual antipathy between Butler and Macmillan. Macmillan regarded his colleague as solemn and priggish; Butler regarded his chief as politically supple to the point of indecency. Large sections of the Conservative Party in the House of Commons had also come to regard Butler with suspicion. They vaguely classified him as a man of the left, who had been lukewarm in his support of the

Suez intervention and was otherwise associated as Home Secretary with soft penal policies.

One of the greatest assets of the earlier part of his career had been the group of gifted young Tories, many of them destined to political prominence, whom he had 'discovered' and whose cause he had espoused immediately after the war. Many of these young men, however, found themselves in less and less sympathy with Butler as the years went on. In this, Powell was no exception. Privately, he had been bitterly critical of Butler's lack of financial realism as Chancellor. Butler, for his part, had long ago come to classify Powell as a 'fanatic' and 'a natural resigner'. Malicious political gossips have it that Butler played some part in creating the state of affairs which had led to Powell's resignation with his two Treasury colleagues in 1958.

On the face of it, therefore, nothing is more surprising than that Powell should have emerged in 1963 as the leader of a group determined to secure the Premiership for Butler. The Conservative Party still lacked a procedure of election for the choice of its leader. The 'customary processes' of consultation between the retiring Prime Minister, members of his Cabinet, the Whips, the Chairman of the 1922 Committee, the party chairman and the backbenchers were still in use. Macmillan's version of these processes was indeed far more thorough than that of any of his predecessors. There were interminable consultations at his hospital bedside. Backbenchers were not only asked whom they liked most but also whom they disliked most.

Many, including Powell, suspected that these in-

vestigations were only the democratic façade for a
carefully-laid scheme to justify passing over Butler
again. When, at the Conservative Party Conference,
Quintin Hogg embarked on a personal publicity drive
of unusual dimensions, involving several appearances
in bathing trunks and culminating in an announcement,
amid frenzied applause from the hall, that he felt it his
duty to abandon his peerage in order to put his services
fully at the disposal of his country, these suspicions
were confirmed. The mildly malicious held that the
signal for this exercise had come from Macmillan's
sickroom. The very malicious added that, although
this was undoubtedly so, it would be naive to suppose
that Macmillan actually intended Hogg to succeed.
The Prime Minister's aim, it was speculated, was to
raise up a formidable alternative to Butler, thereby
indicating the need for a compromise candidate to
reunite the party and opening the way for the appointment of Home.

I have little doubt that Powell shared at least many
of these suspicions. Two days before Home kissed
hands with the Queen the rumour that he had emerged
victorious from the 'customary processes' leaked out,
and Powell took the initiative in summoning a meeting
of colleagues in the late evening to his house in South
Eaton Place. The Chief Whip was also asked to be
present. In spite of the secrecy with which this 'mid-
night conspiracy' was surrounded, Ministers arriving
at the meeting found Press photographers on the
doorstep.

The upshot of this conclave was that a number of
Ministers, whose presence in the government was

widely regarded as essential to its survival, intimated that, in their view, the appointment of Lord Home would be a grievous mistake, and that in spite of the high personal regard in which they held him. Some at least indicated that they would not be prepared to serve under him unless Butler, whom they now regarded as the sole viable alternative, consented to do so.

Macmillan proceeded unmoved with the recommendation of Home. Butler, his most cherished ambition now shattered, responded to an appeal not to make trouble and consented to serve. The entire Cabinet, with the exceptions of Powell and Iain Macleod, placed their services at the new Prime Minister's disposal.

At the time, Powell tenaciously refused to offer any full public explanation of his decision to decline office. An M.P., he rightly argued, is under no obligation to provide public reasons for refusing an appointment. The only clue which he was prepared to vouchsafe was a reminder that he had been strongly opposed to the recent Act of Parliament which authorised the surrender of peerages and by virtue of which, alone, Home was eligible for the Premiership.

There is charm in this interpretation of Powell's behaviour. As a historian of the peerage, he has a deep respect for that institution, and for the hereditary principle generally. Those who opposed Home most vehemently did so on the ground that his choice argued a reversion to the old type of aristocratic, 'enclosed' Conservative Party, that he presented the 'grouse moor image' and that as a 14th Earl he would seem to the Demos to be privileged and effete. The notion of opposing his appointment on the different ground that an ancient earldom imposes obligations too onerous and too honourable to be sacrificed merely for the convenience of finding a Prime Minister has a touch of quaintness about it which would not be displeasing to Powell. His reputation for romanticism in such matters softens an image which is otherwise somewhat harsh.

These feelings probably did have a part in Powell's decision. It is surely incredible, however, that it was a decisive part. Powell knew that the recent arrangements for the renunciations of hereditary peerages had come to stay. His talent for accepting the inevitable is pronounced. Other and more powerful considerations must have had their part, and about these it is possible to speculate.

Those who talked to him at the time recalled the genuine emotion with which he spoke of Butler's disappointment. In spite of the gulf which had long divided them politically, Butler was still Powell's original patron, the man under whose protection he had entered politics, the man who at first distinguished his abilities. Gratitude plays a stronger part in political behaviour than is commonly supposed, and often manifests itself at unexpected moments with unexpected force. The notion that it was responsible, at least in part, for Powell's sudden espousal of Butler's cause cannot, I believe, be excluded.

It may well be that other factors operated on Powell's mind, however unconsciously. For some time, one may suspect, the double role of prophet, dedicated to the thorough re-statement of Conservatism, and member of Macmillan's government, the source of that Conservatism which had to be restated, had put a strain on Powell. The whole atmosphere of his Party had become intensely uncongenial to him.

Home's succession, certainly, offered no great hope of change of the kind which Powell passionately wanted. It is true that Home was generally classified as 'a man of the right', an epithet which was now beginning to be applied to Powell. It was, nevertheless, a totally different kind of 'right' from that which Powell represented. Home's thinking on Commonwealth and foreign policy was still cast in that old-fashioned liberal-imperialist mould from which Powell had escaped. Home had few views on domestic policy, but might be suspected of inclining towards a tradition of Tory paternalism which Powell now strongly rejected. Under suspicion as a reactionary, Home might also be under the considerable temptation to anticipate his critics by throwing himself even more violently into the progressive and expansionist policies of the Macmillan era.

Even without much calculation, Powell may have felt that the time had come to throw off the shackles, to put aside his Ministerial briefcase and mount the prophet's rostrum unencumbered by Cabinet responsibility. The tension between the wish to govern and the wish to preach is still one of the most awkward ingredients in Powell's character.

It is true that when the Tories were defeated at the election of 1964, Powell, after some little contemplation, accepted the offer of a Shadow post. He may have thought that yet another refusal would prove fatal to

his political influence. What he certainly did think—
and made repeatedly clear—was that the freedom to
be properly enjoyed by a Shadow Minister was considerably greater than that which belonged to a Cabinet
Minister. His mind was already made up—if the
functions of educator and policy-maker were to become
incompatible, he would sacrifice immediate political
influence to long-term influence over the mind of his
Party and his country. It was this determination which
explained the uneasy relations which later on developed
between him and his Party Leader, when Heath had
succeeded Home. It was this in the end which led to
the breach of last April.

Powell's departure from the Government in 1963
was therefore a turning point in his career. A few
weeks before it took place he granted me an interview
of considerable length the substance of which was
published in *The Sunday Telegraph*. Since it gives the
best publicly available evidence of the state of his mind
at this critical juncture and since it gives some clue to
the methods by which Powell had reconciled, to his
own intellectual satisfaction, his presence in the Macmillan Government with a radical rejection of almost
all the assumptions on which that Government proceeded the greater part of it is here reproduced.

He begins with the doubts: 'I am worried, deeply
worried,' he says, 'by two widely made assumptions
which seem to dominate our thinking today in a way
which they did not 10 years ago. The first is reflected
in the mood of national self-abasement and pessimism
typified in the July number of *Encounter*; the second

is the habit of looking automatically to government for the solution whenever confronted by any kind of problem.

'Through these attitudes we can so easily slide into thinking that the only way to be rescued from ruin is by stripping ourselves of all our inherited characteristics, jettisoning all typically British methods of conducting life, abandoning all our proven systems of selection and decision-making, and consigning our destiny to the hands of a few omniscient technocrats.

'These attitudes are, in fact, ready-made instruments of persuasion at the disposal of the Labour Party to further its electoral prospects. They oblige even Tory Governments to operate within the framework of an implicitly Socialist public opinion.'

This, as Powell sees it, is the Tory dilemma and the Tory challenge.

National self-depreciation, he contends, is pandered to by the habit of using deceptive or at best irrelevant statistics as whips with which to scourge ourselves. There is, for instance, no revealing conclusion about national decadence to be drawn from the fact—in which Left-wing economists now luxuriate—that Britain's percentage of world trade has declined in the last ten years.

As the European nations have been recovering and new nations entering the arena of world trade, what other statistical effect do people expect? The same arithmetical process has been going on since the beginning of the century and before. And anyhow, what on earth is a percentage share of total world trade supposed to prove about a country's prosperity, progress and well-being?

Another trick of the purveyors of gloom is to record only the depressing aspects of every elementary fact about Britain's geographical and economic position in the world. 'They observe,' says Powell, 'that we are a large population packed into a small space. For them this means that we can easily be destroyed by a ruthless enemy whom we have failed to deter from attack. It never means, what is equally true and far more pertinent to the present, that we have the outstanding economic advantage of having all our resources, human and physical, in close proximity.'

But even if the mood of self-depreciation were well founded, where is the warrant for the belief that State direction is the path of salvation? That this is so prevalent is due to the superstitious reverence with which the technocrats have succeeded in investing themselves. If our progress is to be unfavourably contrasted with that of Germany, might it not be relevant to add that Germany is dedicated to a free enterprise economy? Many people, however, are prepared to believe the technocrats even when what they serve out is against their direct personal experience:

'The people chose,' says Powell, 'to live in the South rather than the North of England: they flocked in obedience to their own calculations of advantage southwards. They were proved abundantly right; they became in consequence richer than they ever had been before, and enjoyed better conditions of life. But now the technocrats say that they ought not to have done it at all, and the people meekly agree.

'Nothing can be more certain than that if the distribution of our population had been planned by a

G

central authority 50 years ago we should have been infinitely worse off than we are now.'

The essence of the Tory faith, says Powell, is the conviction that salvation lies within the grasp of the people themselves; that, by their unhampered pursuit of their own insights, we shall forge ahead in the future just as we advanced in the past.

The State can and must maintain the value of money; it can legitimately pursue a foreign trading policy; it must finance defence and other national and public purposes out of taxation; and it may promote welfare services to modify the harshness of life, and secure basic but rising standards of material comfort to all people. But the State ought not to will specific economic development; it cannot will the good society. It can only set the framework within which society evolves according to its own genius and by means of an infinite series of private decisions directed to private ends but tempered by a rational patriotism and taken in the light of as much accurate information about the nation's activities and their total effect as central agencies like the N.E.D.C. and the N.I.C. can supply.

How then does the Minister see the possibilities open to a Tory in Twentieth-Century government?

He knows that politics is the art of the possible and that institutions which the nation has evolved must be respected even though they arose in part from false doctrine. He is no liberal radical wanting to scrap all the apparatus of government control and start building a free society from scratch. But he believes that two ideas are contending for the soul of Britain: the idea of State Socialism and the idea of freedom, and that, within the limits of what is possible without a counter-revolution, the Government can encourage the forces of freedom. He also sees the politician as a teacher who, by constantly attacking false assumptions, can over the years help to change the climate of opinion.

'Today,' says Powell, 'the Ministry of Health is perforce the central spending authority; I must try to use the power that falls to me as Minister as rationally as I can and with what little foresight is ever vouchsafed to a planner. But I do claim that I have used this power in a way different from that in which it would have been exercised by one of other convictions.

'I have tried to build up and strengthen local agencies within the national system; I have done all that lies in me to strengthen and encourage voluntary effort and the voluntary bodies. I have gone, some would say, to the length of adulation in commending the activities of such independent bodies as the King's Hospital Fund and the Nuffield Trust; I have jealously guarded the frontiers between administration on the one side and the territories of professional knowledge and skill, of scientific research and of commercial enterprise on the other.'

What about education? That, in Powell's opinion, presents far more difficulties than health.

'It is unnatural to the Tory to have to work on the assumption that this activity, which of all others should be an expression of spontaneous national character, can be directed from above; it is repugnant to have to pretend to know the answers to such fatuous questions as how many theologians Britain will need in 1985,

and what proportion they should bear in the interests
of popular happiness to the number of physicists. Yet
the State is the main spending authority, and must
seek to spend rationally.

'It is well that the State education policies should be
controlled by men whose creed teaches them to respect
local, professional and parental opinion and even the
hopes, tastes and desires of the students and pupils
themselves.'

But here Powell allows himself to wonder whether
administrative ingenuity may one day devise a method
of directly endowing students and allowing them by
the free use of their endowments to take an active part
in determining the content of university education.

Powell's convictions are unshaken by the suggestion
that it may be difficult to win an election in the next
year on the basis of a philosophy which deliberately
eschews a programme of bigger and brighter Government intervention all round. He will not be bludgeoned
by the argument that we have proceeded so far on the
road to Socialism that efficiency demands we go the
whole hog. 'Victory will be valueless unless we have
chosen rightly the ground on which to fight.'

V

Defence

No interpretation of a recent political event has
been wider of the mark than that generally advanced of Heath's decision to allocate defence
to Powell in forming his first Shadow Cabinet. The
general view was that the appointment had the purely
negative aim of stopping the *enfant terrible* from talking
about economics, of diverting his energies into an area
where no serious collision with his colleagues was
likely to take place.

Jokes by the score flew around about what would be
likely to happen if Powell applied Powellism to the
organisation of national defence. Gibraltar, it was said,
would be sold to the highest bidder; the Navy would
be leased to I.C.I. It was in the field of economics and
social policy that Powell had made his fundamental
impact on such of the public as had listened to him.
What the public altogether failed to appreciate was
the secondary importance to his whole philosophy of
politics of his distinctive opinions about finance and
trade. They failed to realise, in fact, that the very
foundation of Powellism is a theory of foreign policy

and defence which derives from one event, the traumatic event of Powell's political career, the end of the Indian Empire.

The primary functions of government are to suppress murder and theft at home and to defend its subjects against foreign attacks. Before it is possible to argue rationally about the second function, it is necessary to know who the Government's subjects are, within what limits its jurisdiction stretches. The test of a nation's existence is the willingness of its members, in the last resort, to sacrifice their lives for the sake of defending the collectivity which they together constitute against the danger of falling under foreign rule. In modern conditions, it may be that the test is the even stricter one of their willingness to allow the collectivity itself to be physically and totally destroyed rather than to permit any part of it to pass under alien dominion.

The starting point of Powell's thinking about defence is his conviction that, to all intents and purposes, the limits of the British nation and therefore of the responsibilities of the British government were fundamentally changed by the loss of India in 1947. Until then, Britain was 'a dual polity'. The defence of the Indian Empire was as elementary and sacred a part of the duties of the British state as was the defence of Dover. It was superfluous, it might have proved disturbing, to enquire into the material advantages which the average citizen of the United Kingdom secured from the possession of the Empire. The fact of its existence created obligations which promptly determined the nature and detail of our defence arrangements.

With the ending of the Indian Empire, those obligations ceased. Thenceforward, British defence policy
must be directed exclusively to the defence of these
islands. The implications for it, and for the foreign
policy of which it is an extension, were revolutionary.
It took Powell several painful years of transition, during
some of which he was fiercely resisting the abandonment of British positions in Suez, to reconcile himself
to them.

By the time he joined Heath's Shadow Cabinet his
reconciliation was complete and the extent of his
dramatic conversion known to all his colleagues and
appreciated by none of them more vividly than by
Heath. Far from there being any attempt to neutralise
Powell by directing his mind to defence, the new
leader was appointing him to one of the most crucial
and pressing of missions—the destruction of the
Imperial legend which has so important a part in the
mythology of British Toryism, the conversion of the
Conservative Party to an eventual policy of wholesale
withdrawal from the Near East to the Far East. There
can be no doubt either that Powell relished this task;
he thought of himself as having been entrusted with
a post more congenial to his nature and more in keeping with his ideas than any other which he could
possibly have been offered.

This fact and the general interpretation which he
put upon his task is well illustrated by one of the most
self-revealing interviews which he has ever given, an
interview with Mr. Julian Critchley reported in the
April–June issue of the Bow Group magazine *Cross-
bow*:

JC Would you agree that your appointment as shadow Minister of Defence had an educative purpose? The views you put forward are not those of very many Tory backbenchers!

JEP Well, politics consist very largely in helping people to adjust their mythology to changes in the outside world. It's a painful process, which has to go on all the time, and politics is very largely about this. We have continuously to adjust ourselves to a world not that in which I was born, a world in which there is no longer a British Viceroy and Governor-General on the throne of the Moguls in Delhi. So long did Britain govern India that all the assumptions which derive from governing India are bred into the bone of our thinking and talking. This creates a difficult and also dangerous ambivalence and psychological tension between emotions and observable reality. It is the business of politics to mediate the resolution of such tensions. Let me give an example of the way this mythological view of the world dominates the thinking of us all. Why are we startled by Russian warships in the Mediterranean and not by Russian warships in the Baltic? Answer: because we still think the Mediterranean is the route to India, the life-line of the British Empire—we still think that it is the vital link of that strange, unique, fantastic bi-polar state which was India cum Britain, the spinal cord of which did indeed run through the Mediterranean. Consideration for that spinal cord dominated our policies, from Berlin to Cape Town, during two centuries. So deep in our thinking—and this is my point—in our habitual reactions, does the influence of the vanished past penetrate. You asked, did my appointment have an educative purpose? Of course, all serious politics is—it's rather a pompous word and I don't like it, but I'll accept it in the way you use it—'educational'. You are trying to provide people with words and ideas which will fit their predicament better than the words and ideas which they are using at the moment. This is, to me, what politics is about, and I am sure that Ted Heath, when he asked me, to my great delight, to speak for

the Party on defence, knew very well what my outlook was
on the shape of the present and future world and on Britain's
place in it. It's an outlook which I believe to be close kin
to his own.

The future criterion for deciding on defence arrangements must, in Powell's view, be the requirements of
the security of these islands. Britain is now bereft of
imperial commitments. Arguments which attribute to
her a world role in the maintenance of international
order are merely ghosts from her imperial past. No
such order, in any definable meaning of the term, exists
to be maintained. The United Nations is not an effective instrument for preserving peace or the status quo.
Nations, in these circumstances, have a negative duty
to respect each other's rights; their ultimate positive
duties are exclusively towards themselves.

Looking at the requirements of purely British security, Powell sees as the fundamental heresy of the age
the doctrine, advanced in the famous Sandys White
Paper on Defence in 1957, that strategic necessities
have been altered beyond recognition by nuclear warfare. He makes three points about nuclear strategy
with equal emphasis: the sole value of a nuclear weapon
is to provide a deterrent against attack by another nuclear weapon. Thus the nation which resorts to nuclear
warfare and exposes itself thereby to nuclear reprisal
is, in effect, committing suicide; it will do so only in
response to a threat which is literally worse than death.
Even foreign conquest and occupation for a long period
does not in reality constitute such a threat. It would in
practice be held to be a less serious evil than the
physical destruction of the entire people.

Powell's second point is that, by the same token, no nation will expose itself to the risk of annihilation in order simply to preserve in existence an ally however close. It follows that any defence policy for Britain which relies on the threat of American nuclear reprisals is automatically ruled out. Like other nations, the American people might be supposed by an intending attacker to be willing to take revenge for their own destruction by nuclear attack. The commanders of American nuclear submarines might be willing to compass the destruction of the Soviet Union or a large part of it in response to the certainty that their own country was about to be similarly destroyed. The fact that no intending attacker can wholly dismiss this possibility of revenge is the essence of the deterrent power of the nuclear weapon. Manifestly, however, no attacker will be equally ready to believe that the American people will expose themselves to annihilation in order to preserve the British Isles.

From these two points it follows that the possession of an independent nuclear deterrent is necessary to the security of Britain. Powell, however, attaches equal importance to the possession of conventional forces adequate to resist any conventional attack. The necessity of the nuclear weapon to defence in a nuclear war and its absolute uselessness as a protection against conventional attack are the two foundations of his theory of defence. That theory implies, of course, a total rejection of the idea of a limited nuclear war, and this rejection is made clear in another extract from the Critchley interview:

There is, I am aware, a theory, I usually hear it called 'tactical'; but tactical and strategic are meaningless or ambiguous in this context—there is a theory that you can have a gradation in the use of nuclear weapons and can stop at any particular point. But I don't believe in the 39 steps of Herman Kahn. I don't believe in them, for the significance, even in theory, of the use of the nuclear weapon is its demonstration of the intention to escalate to suicide, to mutual obliteration. Therefore I am still entitled to ask, for what stake will one accept obliteration? In preference to what will one accept obliteration?

JC But the logic of this must lead you inevitably to surrender.

JEP This is where I've said it leads you, if you haven't got conventional arms: to surrender or alternatively to strategic nuclear suicide.

JC Along the lines of American policy?

JEP I am sorry; I can't have been clear, I admit straight away that the possession of a substantial nuclear capability is a powerful and probably absolute deterrent to resort by an enemy to the use of nuclear weapons. This I believe. I do not believe that it is a deterrent to the use of non-nuclear weapons by an enemy, and I do not believe that it is any protection against the use of non-nuclear weapons. I spelt this out once by saying that if we were to replay the film from 1930 onwards, I can detect no point at which, if all the nations playing the game had been armed with nuclear weapons, they would have preferred self-extermination to the risk of what happened. In any case they would have been wrong, as we now know. Even Poland would have been wrong. You will find this a very powerful argument. It is highly indestructible.

In fact, Powell is arguing that the mutually cancelling effect of nuclear weapons has created a state of affairs in which British foreign and defence policy can and must be planned as though nuclear weapons had never been invented. Add to this his conviction that Britain is no longer a power with interests in the Middle East and South East Asia (nor, Powell would add, in Africa either), and his conclusion emerges clearly: Britain's essential interest is to equip herself to make a massive contribution to the defence of Western Europe in a conventional war.

In Powell's eyes, the unavoidable logic of this argument has been ignored by successive British governments, but by none more strikingly than the present government. At one moment, policy has seemed to be based on the assumption that the possession of a nuclear deterrent is enough in itself; at others, the quite inconsistent assumption seems to have been made that the existence of strong or relatively strong NATO or conventional forces is necessary to Britain's safety. Now, while lip service is still paid to our obligations to NATO, the Government has embarked on drastic reductions of conventional armaments, reductions which make nonsense of those obligations. In particular its running down of the Territorial Army has deprived us of the necessary nucleus for any massive military intervention on the continent of Europe.

Britain, then, must think of herself as a European power. Paradoxically, the nuclear revolution has made it necessary for her to revert to essentially the same kind of foreign policy as she assumed before she became a world power. The over-riding object of that policy was to ensure that no hostile country or combination of hostile countries should dominate the continent of Europe as a possible prelude to attacking

Britain, and in particular that no hostile power or combination should control France and the Low Countries. The difference is that at present there is no self-sustaining balance of forces on the continent, so that Britain must actively and constantly intervene in order to preserve the balance. To fail to do this would involve the risk of either Russian encroachment on Western Europe or (an equally unattractive prospect to Powell) the re-emergence of Germany as the dominant power in Europe.

These clear-cut views have been exposed to considerable criticism. Some have urged that Powell is quite wrong to argue that a limited nuclear war is impossible. They admit that the use of nuclear tactical weapons on the battlefield would afford little advantage to Britain and the Western European powers as a means of counteracting Russian strength. In conventional warfare, the advantage (still estimated at about 4 to 1) is with the defence; in tactical nuclear warfare the defence has no such superiority. They contend, however, that it might be possible to use comparatively large nuclear weapons for the destruction of particular cities without thereby embarking on total nuclear war. They envisage, for instance, that if the West was using a conventional war in Europe it might decide to 'take out' a single Russian city by nuclear attack; Russia might respond by 'taking out' a single Western European city. The result would be a war of nerves in which each side tried to convey to the other its willingness to go further along the road of nuclear war.

It is possible to concede that this argument has some

truth in it without allowing that it makes any fundamental difference to Powell's thesis. A course such as
this would, to say the least, be highly dangerous to a
power as vulnerable as Britain to nuclear assault. The
possibility of pursuing it would be no substitute for
strong conventional forces.

The majority of Powell's critics (most strongly
represented in the Conservative Party) concentrate,
however, on his advocacy of total withdrawal East of
Suez. They contend that this will mean the abandonment of considerable British economic assets and might
lead to essential raw materials such as oil passing under
enemy control. They also contend that this policy
ignores the danger of allowing the balance of power
in other continents to be destroyed by an aggressor
who may eventually make a bid for world domination.

To these criticisms Powell's answers are clear. The
cost of maintaining bases in the Indian Ocean, the
Persian Gulf and South East Asia is not the counterpart or precondition of the return Britons receive from
their investments in those areas. Middle Eastern and
Asian countries will still have a commercial interest in
selling their raw materials to the West even when
Western power is withdrawn. If they are physically
prevented from doing so by the enemies of the West
in wartime, there are plenty of alternative sources of
supply open to us (e.g. the United States and Nigeria
for oil).

Finally, and most important of all, Powell is profoundly convinced that Western attempts to intervene
in the maintenance of the balance in other continents
are foredoomed to failure. They cannot easily be

militarily effective (witness American intervention in Vietnam) and they are bound to arouse local antagonism which must powerfully diminish if it does not totally destroy the military advantages of a 'Western presence'. In this connection, Powell's feelings about the fatuity of the Vietnam war and his regret for the constant moral support which our supposed economic dependence on America has forced the Labour Government to give it might well be taken into account by many of his bitterer critics on the Left. In this respect, he is nearer to them than they are to Mr. Wilson.

No feat of tightrope walking in recent British political history has been more remarkable than Powell's handling of his double function of educating the Conservative Party about defence and representing its official policy against Labour. A powerful section of Powell's colleagues, including of course pre-eminently Sir Alec Douglas Home, are firmly identified with a policy of maintaining British power East of Suez. It is the natural instinct of Conservatives to cheer whenever British troops are sent abroad and barrack the British Government when they are withdrawn. The further away they are sent, the more content the rank and file of the Party becomes.

As Shadow Minister of Defence, Powell was obliged bitterly to attack the very policy of withdrawal East of Suez which he was recommending to his own supporters. The methods by which he reconciled his conscience were wholly defensible intellectually. Withdrawals must be properly timed if they are not to lead to anarchy and the abandonment of obligations of

honour. In particular, Powell, remembering the mas-
sacres in the Punjab, is in principle opposed to announcing precise dates of withdrawal well in advance
of the event and without imposing any conditions
regarding the kind of local settlement which will ensue.

He would probably have made this point even had
he not been under the necessity of finding some argument consistent with his own principles which would
justify him in opposing the Government. Finally,
Labour's policy of withdrawal has been part of a
general and drastic reduction in military preparedness
all over the world, involving the considerable weaken-
ing of Britain's position in Europe. Attacking this
policy is, of course, wholly congenial to Powell.

Nevertheless, the tensions have remained. Representing a Party while educating it is the hardest of
political tasks. Essentially, Powell's aim has been to
divert the patriotic fervour of the Conservative Party
from the useless and disastrous task of defending the
last outposts of a deserted Empire to the essential task
of defending Europe. At the outset, he had the full
support of his Leader in this perilous mission. As time
went on, and difficulties arose in other fields, there is
no doubt that that support began to waver.

It is possible to speculate that Powell's feeling that
his defence policy might be betrayed was not the least
of the factors which induced him to speak his mind on
other subjects with less than scrupulous regard for the
convenience of his colleagues.

Equally, not the least of the dangers which have
come about from his rift with those colleagues has been
a perceptible tendency on their part to differentiate

themselves from him (possibly with one eye on the ever militant rank and file of the Tory Party) by demanding the maintenance of British bases everywhere. Those sections of the party most inclined to favour Powell's views on immigration are often those least inclined to favour what they regard as his 'leftish' tendencies over defence. Party tacticians are adept at turning such calculations to advantage without too much regard to the ultimate demands of national and party interest.

VI

The Economics of Powell

'OFTEN when I am kneeling down in church, I think to myself how much we should thank God, the Holy Ghost for the gift of capitalism.' This remark recently made by Powell at a private luncheon of tough-minded lobby correspondents sums up perfectly the spirit of his campaign for the reform of the economic doctrines of the Conservative Party. There was not a touch of irony or even of conscious exhibitionism in it. He sees in the operation of what he regards as the natural laws of economics the hand of providence.

Accordingly, attempts to interrupt these laws have at the best the quality of blasphemy and at the worst the quality of sacrilege. He thinks of economic planners as being engaged, innocently or deliberately, in the celebration of a perpetual black mass. God, in His infinite mercy, has contrived a constitution of things designed to enable men to promote His glory and improve their own state without undue exercises either of self-sacrifice or of rational forethought. To despise this boon is not merely unspeakable folly, it also argues profound impiety. Those who make the attempt are constituting themselves as providence and will suffer the inevitable nemesis.

Over the last three years, Powell has conveyed these theological views to the public in a series of speeches each of which has had strong topical relevance. He has condemned the National Plan, the Prices and Incomes Policy and Government schemes for giving special assistance to the economic development of particular regions. His attacks, however, have not been concentrated exclusively on government. He has not spared those industrialists who have co-operated with government. Powell believes not only that it is legitimate to buy in the cheapest market and sell in the dearest, but that it is positively immoral to do otherwise.

Nothing has attracted more bitter reproaches from him than the techniques by which the Government has persuaded employers and workers alike to subordinate their private interests to the Government's view of what is required by the public interest. He has seen this as a dangerous constitutional tendency as well as a presumptuous affront to the natural laws of economics. People have been persuaded to behave in ways in which the law does not require them to behave by being induced to feel a sense of guilt whenever their behaviour conflicts with the wishes of Ministers of the Crown—wishes which, as Powell maintains, have no more authority than those of the private citizen until they have received the sanction of Parliament.

Powell believes that this no-man's-land between what is the province of the law and what belongs to the discretion of the individual is the decisive area of political conflict. A recurring theme of his speeches has been the insidious character of the methods by which the sphere of public power is now being extended. A Government which tried by statute to nationalise all the means of production and distribution would at least have the merit of acting directly, of challenging openly the assumptions of the free society. A society thus warned would at least have the opportunity of resisting those who intend to master it. Moderate socialism, on the other hand, proceeds by stealth.

Powell regards nothing as being so dangerous as the profusion of committees of industrialists, trades unionists and civil servants concerned with planning, by voluntary co-operation, the nation's economic development. They represent the contemporary, pale version of fascist corporatism. Their object is to subdue all the surviving centres of private resistance to public power. Through them, the State operates both on the consciences and the ambitions of the ordinary citizen. These semi-official institutions even become, in Powell's view, powerful sources of corrupt patronage. Business men receive public honours for acquiescing in the policies of government and co-operating in their execution.

Powell's economic doctrines are unintelligible except on the assumption, which he explicitly makes, that an attempt is afoot to impose a detailed and comprehensive kind of economic planning on Britain. He is firmly convinced that this attempt has already largely succeeded, so largely that any operation designed to stem the tide must also aim at turning it back. To this extent, he is, inevitably, in relation to economic policy, a counterrevolutionary. In his view, it will not suffice to say 'thus far and no further'. Already, large areas of the surviving private sector of the economy are distorted and rendered inefficient by the operations of public control. Nothing short of a fundamental revision of the economy in the direction of competitive enterprise will suffice. The extension of public control still further would be a more logical and even might prove to be a more workable policy than sticking to the status quo.

Powell opposes to the fashionable collectivism, a theory of free enterprise which is almost as rigorous in character. He believes himself to be engaged in an ideological battle between two clearly defined systems. One of them, he thinks, is bound to produce stagnation and poverty at the cost of tyranny; the other will produce a natural adjustment of interests not perfect but representing the nearest possible approximation to perfection.

At no point, of course, is he attacking the supremacy of the public interest. His contention is that the public interest will best be secured by the pursuit, within the limits of the rule of law, of individual interests. Attention must therefore concentrate on what Powell's view of the limits of those interests are. What, in fact, is his philosophy of State intervention in economics?

Among his recent utterances, the best source of illumination on this question is a speech he delivered to the Cambridge Union on the 6th February, 1968.

The occasion was congenial to him, for it called for no particular concessions to his audience. Powell is

still most at home in debates with academics. His chief
opponent, Professor Galbraith, the popular American
economist, was well chosen to bring out the distinctive
qualities in Powell's thinking.

Galbraith is an exponent of the idea of managed
capitalism. He believes that doctrinal disputes about
the respective spheres of private and public enterprise
are wholly irrelevant. He thinks that competition is an
illusion. He contends that the great industrial corpora-
tions have many of the qualities of the State—that far
from responding to public demand they habitually
determine it and that, unless they could do so effectively, it would be impossible for them to survive in
view of the vastness of their investment programmes
and the consequent need to predict the state of the
market with unfailing precision. Galbraith's ideas tend
exactly towards that system of close co-operation between government and private industry which Powell
regards as so sinister.

The proposition which Powell was called on to
defend was that the State could properly regulate
economic affairs but could not properly intervene in
them. He demurred only slightly to this formulation,
doubting the perfection of the terms regulation and
intervention as means of distinguishing the two types
of State activity concerned, but not questioning that
there were two such types and that a choice in principle
between them was essential. His argument is worth
examining in detail.

Powell starts with a lengthy and lucid definition of
the alternatives:

'That which is here described as regulatory, is by nature general in its effect. When the State regulates, it says "Take note that all persons must comply with the following rules and requirements." For instance, it says, "you may not employ persons below a given age, whatever the manufacture is. That you may not employ women other than in certain defined conditions. That whatever it is that you are doing or manufacturing, wherever you are doing it, there are certain requirements of health and safety with which you must comply." Having laid down those universal requirements, the citizen or the groups of citizens are thereafter free to decide what they shall or shall not manufacture, where they shall sell it, where they shall manufacture it and so on. In the planning regulation, the State says, "In this area, thus defined, there shall be no industry." Take note. But it leaves open to the citizen, thenceforward, to establish an industry in the rest of the available area, to which that prohibition does not apply, so that when the State is regulating, it is issuing general commands, or more commonly, general prohibitions, but within the framework which those commands and prohibitions set up, the individuals acting through the market, acting upon the indices of prices and profit, take their own decisions.

'The honourable member who has just spoken referred to the activity of the State in attempting to maintain a stable price of money. Now here we can very clearly distinguish a regulatory from an interventionist behaviour. The State may use the powers available to it to maintain a general balance between total demand and total production. While leaving the

content of that production in its infinite variety to be
determined by the population as a whole, by all the
processes of the market. Such is the regulatory function of the State in regard to the economy. It lays
down general prescriptions, but initiative remains elsewhere.

'Now when the State intervenes, it acts in the opposite way. When it intervenes, it says "there shall be
such and such a steel works in such and such a place.
There shall be industry and employment in such and
such a part of the country. We will ensure not only
that industry is not established in area A, but that it
is established, and that industry of a particular kind is
established in area B." Now this, the interventionist
activity of the State, is different in kind and different
in its effects, for it attracts to the State, it vests in the
State the essential initiative and power of decision, and
it makes the State responsible for directing, in detail,
the economic activity of all the members of the community. So here there is an absolutely vital and valid
distinction between two types of State action which
I hope the House will accept. . . .'

Powell goes on to say that regulation is in the very
nature of the State. It is merely, in fact, an extension
of the principle of the community. It is a government's
business to make laws which apply generally to its
citizens and are concerned with that part of their lives
which can rightly be subjected to the authority of
common rule. Within the bounds of these laws, however, the individual is free in a regulated society to
make his own plans, to calculate and pursue his own

interests. The customer is free to buy what he likes where he likes, and the manufacturer to consider whether what he is offered for his services makes it worthwhile having it. The structure and functioning of an economy of this kind are the product of an infinite variety of private decisions.

When the State proceeds from regulation to intervention, however, it is substituting its own will for the will of its citizens as expressed in this complex of private judgments and actions. No doubt, in so doing, it presents its own will as the embodiment of the general will of society, but the identification is in practice fraudulent. Inevitably, the interventionist decisions of the State are the responsibility of a small body of men in Whitehall—ultimately the responsibility of the Cabinet. An autocracy is thus substituted for the democracy of the market.

Powell is forced to recognise, however, that most of the State's activities produce, in some degree, economic consequences. May they not therefore properly be defined as economic activities? Decisions, for instance, about the size of the Army cannot reasonably be described as regulatory in character. They involve actual administrative actions, and actions which can obviously have a decisive effect on economic life.

Having established, at least to his own satisfaction, that the State should act only in a regulatory manner when concerned with economics and having postulated a large non-economic area in which the State must be free to act in an interventionist manner, Powell must now consider what the distinguishing characteristics of an economic decision are. He continues thus:

'. . . By an economic decision I mean this: I mean a choice between alternatives, which can be compared on a common and normally on a monetary scale.

'Let us apply that to alternative cases. The State has decided that for the national defence, it is necessary to provide a certain number of warships—of a certain character. Now it would be of no interest if the State were informed but for the same money, or less, you could have a large number of alternative purchases. It would be of no interest if they were informed that for the same money you could, for example, have a given number of schools or a given number of hospitals. The reply would be, "That is not the point. That comparison does not meet the purpose with which the State is engaging in this activity. It is doing so for the purpose of national defence, and that is a purpose which is not commensurable, on the same money-scale, with the other incommensurable purposes, such as education, public health—which the State may pursue."

'Now quite different is the nature of an economic decision. Nobody prefers, for the sake of it, to mine 200,000 tons of coal a year, if the same amount of power and energy can be obtained more cheaply. In an economic decision we weigh alternatives, alternative forms of satisfaction, on the common scale of cost, price or profit, so that the essence of economic decisions, the essence of an economic purpose, is that we

are aiming at a satisfaction which we are always prepared to commute for another satisfaction, if that is
able to be obtained at less effort, and is more attractive.
The economic decision is thus always substituting one
bundle of satisfactions for another, all of which can
be measured off on a common monetary scale, and
thus when the State intervenes, and intervenes for
economic purposes, then the State is essentially taking
a decision about the satisfactions which its citizens shall
enjoy.

'And here the great gulf is crossed which this motion
seeks to emphasise. It passes, the State passes, where it
intervenes economically, from the pursuit of common
purposes. The provision of common defence; the provision of common amenities; the provision of a common
system of law and administration. It passes over to
actions which pre-determine what satisfactions its
citizens shall and shall not have.'

Powell proceeds to illustrate the consequences of
interventionism by reference to the Government's
National Plan. By deciding on a four per cent per
annum increase in national growth over the next five
years, the State has already wrested from its citizens a
fundamental decision about how they shall live. Elsewhere he pours scorn on a complaint from the Prime
Minister that past increases of productivity have been
cancelled out by increased demands for leisure. Why,
he asks, should a government dictate to the community
what balance it should strike between the advantages
of increased material prosperity and the advantages of
more free time?

In this respect, there is, incidentally, a marked difference between Powell's approach to the whole question of economic policy and that of the majority of his colleagues in the Conservative Party and not least, perhaps, that of its leader. The burden of Conservative complaint has, on the whole, been that Socialist planning will not achieve the purpose of increased growth, that it will fail to induce the degree of effort needed to sustain an ever-expanding economy and to produce ever-increasing wealth. Powell does not exclude the idea that it is legitimate to choose relative poverty plus greater idleness as an alternative to economic expansion. It is no more the business of the State to force people to be prosperous than it is to condemn them to poverty.

Even assuming, however, that the merits of ever-increasing production go unchallenged, Powell goes on, in his Cambridge Union speech, to point out that the planners are perforce driven to determine the character of the kind of production in which industry shall engage.

They are forced to decide not only how much shall be available to the people to consume, but also what they shall consume. Even the most indicative of planners, he insists, cannot confine himself merely to saying that national production shall increase by four per cent.

If that observation is to be anything more than a mere incantation, he must determine what shall be produced. He must go about setting targets for particular industries and urging, bribing or forcing them to achieve those targets. Planning therefore involves a

still further usurpation of popular choice. It is as the
enemy of choice that it is primarily to be condemned.
Yet it is open to other condemnations as well. Even
supposing that the commands of Government are
designed with the intention of coinciding with the
wishes of the people as they would be expressed in a
free market, Government plans will in their very nature
prove inefficient.

'State interventions will always, by nature, be based
on a totally inadequate supply of information, inadequate in quantity and inadequate in promptitude. We
can see the consequences, we can trace examples which
illustrate this in the history of planned industries and
the attempts to plan the economy in this country and
elsewhere in the last twenty years. I'm prepared to
take, for instance, it's been referred to earlier in this
debate—Fuel Policy.

'One thing has been common to all the State
Fuel Policies which we've had since the war,
whether Conservative or Socialist, to all the
policies which have attempted to indicate, even more
to lay down what ought to be the sources of power
for our economy, and that thing which has been
common to them is that they have all been proved to
be hopelessly and utterly wrong within a short time of
being framed. So much so that if they had been persisted in and had been carried through (and presumably the object of a plan, or an intervention must be to
carry it out) they would have brought ruin upon the
economy. All the major developments in the Fuel
Economy in the last twenty years have been

perceived and have been taken account of last by the State.

'The State has been the last to give up obsolete plans, to admit its former errors and to recognise the new possibilities, over and over and over again. And last of all, when in the early 1960s elaborate Fuel Policies which presumably are designed to be implemented were being drawn up in complete ignorance or oblivion of the immense importance of North Sea natural gas.

'That's not the only example—the whole history is strewn with them. One process after another—the Lurgi process in the gas industry has been introduced and has been imposed just at the time when everybody else knew that it was becoming obsolete. There can never be that collection, that continuous collection, that rapid collection and digestion of all the infinite variety of economic facts, bearing upon investment decisions, bearing upon buying and selling, imports and exports if that decision is going to be taken centrally, which is what is meant by being taken by the State. And once the decision is taken by the State it takes long enough to unmake, it takes long enough to disprove because this little group of men who are politicians have attached their political reputation to the White Paper in which the inadequate information digested in the light of political prejudice has been laid down as a policy for economic intervention.

'It is of the very nature of State economic intervention that it is bound to ignore the vast majority of irrelevant facts, because it simply can't cope with

them. That it is bound to be influenced by the factors
which do influence the State in a democratic society.
Political prejudice, political influence and, thirdly, that
it will be longest and slowest in modifying and admitting error, when it becomes eventually an unavoidable
solution.'

Powell now inserts an important qualifying clause:
he is not contending that the operation of the free
market will in itself secure a perfect satisfaction of all
human desires. Any politician who offers such a pana-
cea must be either a fool or a fraud. He is contending
simply that over a large sphere of life (that part of it
which can accurately be described as economic) there
is a choice between submitting choices to the determination of the market and allowing them to be made
by an omnipotent central authority. He is arguing that
the first method is infinitely preferable in that it will
secure a far closer approximation to the intended
result than the second.

Finally, Powell turns to the crux of Galbraith's case,
which also represents the commonest line of criticism
of the economics of Powellism. He considers the argument that the competitive system is now an illusion,
that the market is dominated by large monopolistic
or semi-monopolistic concerns which have many of the
attributes of the State and which in particular create
rather than obey public taste. He is prepared to admit
that, up to a point, there is truth in this proposition.
If so, he cries 'Thank God' that these organisations
are private, that there is some independent power
(the power of government) which can regulate

their activity. The very strength of these concerns is a case for keeping them strictly separate from government.

To unite economic power of this magnitude to the supreme political power of the State is to leave the public at the mercy of a two-headed monster. The State must remain free to exercise its regulative functions over these giants. It must not be allowed to augment its own strength by acquiring theirs; they must not be allowed to corrupt its independence by seizing a privileged share in the shaping of public policy.

Yet Powell declines to admit that the trend towards monopoly and the extinction of competition has gone so far as Galbraith suggests. The great manufacturing combinations, even when they appear to control or virtually to control the domestic market in the products they make can and ought to be subjected to international competition. What is more the customer exercises his choice, not only between the competing makers of the same kind of product but also between different products. You have only to look, Powell contends, at the financial columns of the Press to see how effective this choice is. Daily, companies are obliged to reduce their dividends, they may even be forced into bankruptcy, by their failures to meet public demands. State concerns alone are exempted from this discipline, for they can repair their losses out of the tax-payers' pocket.

There is no question, therefore, of an inevitable drift towards a concentration of economic power. There is a genuine and clear-cut choice between two systems;

the system of direct state intervention and that of state regulation of a free economy. Powell urges us to opt for the second on these grounds:

'It is a system which retains the power of the state to serve and to protect the individual citizen, and it is a system which places an enormous wealth of information culled from all the quarters of the world at the disposal of those who are deciding, in however exalted or however humble a station, how they shall apply their efforts for the best of themselves, for the best of their family, and thereby for the best of their country.'

These, then, are the fundamentals of Powell's economic thought. Manifestly, there is nothing original about them. They are a statement, in an extremely simplified form, of the doctrines of classical liberalism. They are exposed to all the objections to which those doctrines have been exposed by over a century of critical examination both from right and left. Powell commonly does not address himself to the more formidable of these objections, contenting himself, as a politician may be forgiven for doing, with disposing of such as fall easy prey to his superior critical gifts. This neglect of a whole vast area of argument is a recurring source of irritation to those who look at his pronouncements with a critical eye.

A case in point is his acceptance, hook, line and sinker, of what is in fact the economic counterpart of the extreme version of the classical liberal principle of the rule of law—not simply the principle that laws should be applied equally to those to whom they are

I

to be applied but the doctrine that they should, at any rate as far as economics is concerned, be general and largely abstract in character. In the economic sphere, Powell appears to subscribe almost without reservation to the theory that the State must confine itself to making and enforcing general rules. He cites, as an instance of this, the proposition that it would be legitimate for the State to forbid the establishment of new industries in a particular area altogether, but that it would not be legitimate for the State to decide that some industries should be permitted in that area whereas others should not.

This rule is 'general' in that it applies to the whole population; it is particular in that it distinguishes between some places and others. A law which related to some industries and not others would also be particular, but it also might be argued to be general in its application to the community at large. Everyone would be equally subjected to its limitations, everyone, in theory, would be equally eligible for its privileges.

In practice, of course, it would bear and be intended to bear more heavily on some sections of the population than others, but unless some arbitrary limitation, such as that of hereditary succession, were imposed on those engaged in the privileged industries, it could be argued that all members of the population were equally free to enter them. States are not accused of departing from the rule of law when they confer special rights and impose special obligations on civil servants, arising from the particular functions of these people in society. The traditional argument is that everyone is free to apply

for membership of the civil service and that, to this
extent, the law may be said to be binding equally on
the whole community.

Was it wrong for Parliament to regulate the conditions of service in the catering wages industry? If
legislation as specific as this is tolerable, why should
a vast quantity of legislation and potential legislation
of the kind to which Powell objects be rejected on the
grounds of its particularity?

Most acts of parliament are in fact concerned with
adjusting the interests of particular sections of the
community to each other. In a sense they apply to the
whole community, since they do not arbitrarily exclude
any member of it. In reality, they apply to carefully
defined sections of society.

It is one thing to say that laws should be predictable
and that for that reason they should be comparatively
infrequent. It is one thing to say that in making them
the legislator should not be corrupt, that is to say that
he should not be diverted from the public good by
arbitrary preferences for one class of subject over another. It is quite another thing to argue, as Powell
sometimes seems to argue, that the legislator must
never apply himself to the task of reconciling particular
interests.

This position can be maintained in the last resort
only on the basis of a fundamentally un-Tory theory—
that of the separation of powers. It is a theory which
lays it down that legislation should be abstract in character—that it should relate to individuals conceived
in isolation from their social environment, that it
should concern itself, as Disraeli put it when attacking

this dogma, 'with the rights of man' rather than 'with the rights of Englishmen'.

A more serious objection to Powell's argument, particularly as developed in this debate, is its syllogistic character. He distinguishes between the non-economic and the economic activities of the State, conceding the legitimacy of direct State action in the first case and contending that in the second the principle of regulation should prevail.

When it comes to the point, however, Powell is found arguing that the nature of an economic decision is that it is one which permits a choice between two alternative means of satisfaction, which choice can be expressed in monetary terms.

He takes defence as a classical example of a non-economic activity. Has he not heard of the catch phrase of the '30s 'butter or guns'? The choice between a high degree of national security to be achieved by a high degree of public expenditure and a high degree of personal welfare to be achieved either by low taxation or great public expense on the social services has always been one of the central themes of political controversy in Britain. Today, the choice between a considerable increase in public expenditure on the police and the present comparatively poor level of public order is another such theme. Both these choices are expressible and indeed habitually expressed in monetary terms. Presumably both of them, on a strict interpretation of Powell's opinions, should be left to the arbitrament of the market.

Powell, of course, would reply to this absurdity by

saying that national defence and the maintenance of
public order are both in their nature communal activities, but how would he proceed to define a communal
activity? There are those who would maintain (and
Powell is certainly one of them) that proper communal
activity includes the maintenance of a high standard of
education and a high standard of national health and
housing. There are those who would go further and
argue that they involve the maintenance of a high
average standard of living. It may be that direct state
intervention is not the right method of achieving any
of these ends, but it cannot be argued that it can be
excluded on the doctrinaire ground that these ends,
being economic in character, can never properly be
pursued by direct government action.

Fundamentally, Powell believes in what the early
Benthamites called 'the automatic identification of interests'. He contends that the free pursuit of private
gain will, over a large if ill-defined area of life, produce
the maximum social good. He believes that this will
come about by the force of the market which will
produce the most efficient possible division of labour.
It will be the interest of all producers to produce as
cheaply as possible; all consumers, therefore, will be
served as cheaply as possible. Those who can satisfy public need will thrive, those who fail to satisfy it will perish.

Powell's critics have tended to fasten on the un-
reality of this Utopian conception. By so doing, they
have grievously weakened their case, and he has, in
fact, found little difficulty in making mincemeat of
many of them. Of course, the system is not perfect,
but he never maintained that it was—only that it was

a far closer approximation to perfection than the alternative. Of course, the market is not perfect, but there is far more effective competition within it than the critics are willing to concede. For all his sophistication, Professor Galbraith is fundamentally incapable of recognising as a market anything which does not take place in a village square against a background of face to face haggling over price. There are, however, far more formidable objections to Powell's restatement of classical liberalism than this.

The fundamental fallacy of that doctrine is the priority which it gives to the rights and interests of the individual qua consumer over his rights and interests qua producer. It is not to be assumed automatically (Powell would agree) that that man will be happiest who consumes most of what he wants to consume at the cheapest possible price. If the cost at which he achieves this state is that of submitting himself as a producer to the forces of a ruthless competitive system which may oblige him to live where he does not want to live and to work harder than he wishes to work, he will not count himself the gainer. As a consumer he will avail himself gladly of all the advantages of a free economy; as a producer he may fiercely resent its encroachments on his liberty.

This is no abstract conflict. It is part of the ordinary run of policy discussion. The classic example of it from recent history is the controversy over retail price maintenance over which Edward Heath made his reputation. There can be no doubt that Powell himself approved strongly of the legislation which Heath introduced on this point. It was wholly in keeping with Powellite principles. What could be a more monstrous infringement of the principles of a free economy than the practice which this legislation forbade?

It was directed against the arrangements which producers habitually made with each other to fix the prices at which their goods could be sold by retailers. It operated to prevent any economies in the running of retail shops from being passed on to the customer in the shape of lower prices. Wherever it has become effective, the Act has led to a marked intensification of competition between shopkeepers and often to substantial reductions in prices.

Nevertheless, the passage of the Act was resisted vigorously by important sections of the Conservative Party. Of all the arguments they deployed the one which is most emotive in character was their contention that it would drive a great many small shopkeepers rapidly and cruelly out of trade. The supermarkets, which could afford more efficient methods of sale, would crush the village shopkeeper into the dust. Opponents of the Bill pointed to a great variety of moving reasons for keeping a small shop. Many such shops, they said, provided a stable living for the disabled or the elderly. Some critics even pointed to the alleged social value of the small entrepreneur—traditionally supposed to be a stabilising influence and, incidentally, also a Conservative voter.

Many of these arguments were wholly unpersuasive, some manifestly fraudulent, yet they did represent genuine public anxieties. A great many people felt, rightly or wrongly, that by the operation of this Act they would be suddenly deprived of their legitimate expectations. It is true that up to a point these expectations had been built up at the expense of the community at large. All inefficient producers enjoying the benefits of restrictive practices live at the expense of consumers, some of whom, no doubt, in their capacity as producers, are living in precisely the same way. The question is whether it is legitimate for Government to attempt to strike some kind of balance between these conflicting interests or to base itself firmly on the dogma that the customer's interest always has priority.

A Conservative in the Burkean tradition, believing that a large part of the function of the State is to adjust interests, would take the first view, though this would not necessarily lead him to oppose all innovations which might cause immediate injury to some section of the public. Such a Conservative would at least feel justified in making the calculation—in weighing the advantages of maintaining a particular form of social life against its economic cost; Powell would presumably regard any such calculation as wholly irrelevant to the business of government. Yet, where are the moral grounds on which this assumption is made?

Certainly, it is not self-evident that a society organised exclusively for the benefit of consumers will be either happier or more virtuous than one founded on the attempt to adjust as many discernible interests to each other as possible.

Another characteristic of Powell's economic thought, and one which again is distressing to those brought up in the central tradition of English conservatism, is his tendency, in attacking dirigist policies, to assume that any degree of public control leads almost unavoidably to total public control. This enables him to denounce comparatively small measures of State intervention as though they were proposals for the total submergence of freedom.

The habit is loosely described as 'taking things to their logical conclusion', but the element of dedicated logic in it is in fact relatively small. It is true of course, as Powell never ceases to point out, that controls tend to proliferate—that to control the supply of bacon effectively it sometimes becomes necessary to control the supply of eggs as well. In his earlier, One Nation days, Powell recognised, however, that it was always possible for society to stop this process short by an exercise of will. His philosophy of State action in relation to economics was then far more truly Conservative than it now is.

He started with the assumption of a totally free economy. This, so to speak, was a natural state of things, which must be preserved or restored at every point, unless an over-riding social interest demanded some limitation of freedom. If such an interest could be proved, Powell believed that the processes of the free economy could properly be interrupted, if necessary even by direct State action such as import controls. In particular, he attached importance to the right of the State deliberately to slow down economic change for humanitarian reasons.

These decisive qualifying clauses have since receded into the background. Powell seems more and more obsessed with the radical passion for certitude, with the search for clear-cut lines of demarcation between what belongs and what does not belong to government, lines so well defined that they will dispense with the need for the exercise of practical judgment. He sees the seeds of a totalitarian state in every instance of administrative control of the economy and even in every example of discriminatory control exercised by statute rather than ordinance. He is perpetually visiting the sins of the full-grown monster on the embryo. This is an effective debating technique, but it is intellectually unsatisfying.

Powell's rigid principles of economic policy, if treated as a handbook of practical statesmanship, would turn out to be positively dangerous. Yet, as his political career shows, he is not in practice a doctrinaire. That blessed reservation about the 'politically possible' is always at hand to rescue him from the strict consequences of his beliefs. If he were to become Leader tomorrow of a victorious Conservative Party, there is a quite serious danger that he will be in practice not nearly radical enough in his reorganisation of the economy. As always, his passion for administration could be counted on to temper his liberal principles.

The language of political persuasion is always exaggerated. Powell's overwhelming conviction is that the Conservative Party—which sometimes in its history has emphasised authority—must now emphasise liberty. This is an empirical response to the demands of the age. It is not reasonable to expect the practical politician to express his point of view in the carefully balanced language of a political philosopher. What he asserts on the platform as eternal principles he knows, in the study, to be short-hand descriptions of expedient policies.

Philosopher statesmen have not been rare in British politics, but they have generally succeeded in keeping their two functions more distinct than Powell keeps his. His most passionate political pronouncements tend to be couched in academic language, and this intensifies the impression that his views are intolerably rigid and even at times Utopian. The result is some of the most distinctive and engaging pieces of contemporary oratory. (He is a far better speaker than any leading Conservative politician with the possible exceptions, in a totally different vein, of Iain Macleod and Quintin Hogg.)

At times, however, he seems almost to be subordinating content to the exigencies of style, and the style is one which imposes precision where precision is impossible.

Such are Powell's principles of economic policy. They have been applied with a high degree of consistency to the discussion of such topics as Prices and Incomes Policy and the future of the trade unions.

In origin, the Prices and Incomes Policy was a Tory concept. Macmillan, it has been said, handed this stick of dynamite to his Chancellor of the Exchequer, Selwyn Lloyd, who, with characteristic innocence, took it to be a bar of chocolate. The prevailing fallacy of the twilight of the Macmillan administration—what might be described as its 'Berlin bunker' era—was this doctrine which had already developed far by the time the Socialists came to power.

The argument ran thus: It is necessary to have full employment and also necessary to have a high standard of living. Full employment creates a shortage of labour which inflates wages and, therefore, inflates prices as well. This necessitates the repeated application of stringent financial policies designed to correct the balance between money and total production. The economy therefore is subject to continual vicissitudes which are damaging to the prospect of constant growth. To make wages march hand in hand with growth requires a constant policy of conscious control, whether voluntary or imposed by the State. What is more, it is not enough to ensure that the total of national wages does not exceed the total of national production. The surplus which is available for distribution in wages and other incomes must be so distributed as to foster necessary productive activity and to discourage what is less useful. Conscious control must to that extent try to reproduce the characteristics of a free economy based on supply and demand.

The Conservatives, it is true, were chary of pressing these arguments to their logical conclusion. The National Incomes Commission was an advisory body whose function was held to be the representation of the public conscience in matters relating to wages and salaries. It was a kind of Banquo's ghost to sit in a hitherto vacant seat at the industrial conference table. It was there to remind both sides in trade disputes that there was a third factor to be considered, the public interest.

It was not surprising that under Labour this policy developed into a full-scale attempt to control prices and incomes, that a powerful board under the august chairmanship of Mr. Aubrey Jones was established to apply it, and that, eventually, compulsory powers were sought to restrain wage claims in conformity with its recommendations.

From its very beginning under the Tories this exercise in incomes control was repugnant to Powell, though not so repugnant as to prompt his resignation from the Government which had embarked on it. Powell has two salient criticisms of the Prices and Incomes Policy.

In the first place, he believes that, in its present form, it is bound to be totally ineffective. Like most other liberal economists, he delights in exposing the sheer impotence of government planning. As at present practised, he finds the Prices and Incomes Policy to be literal nonsense. It is like pouring water into a bottomless pail or squeezing a ball at one point merely to make it bulge at another. What determines the cost of living is the relationship between the amount of money available for expenditure on consumption and the number of things available to be consumed. If the Government can succeed in arbitrarily restricting the prices of particular goods or services, it can achieve nothing, by so doing, except a false rendering of public demand. What the public most needs will be kept artificially cheap; expenditure on what it does not need so much will be artificially inflated.

By pursuing simultaneously a policy of financial squeeze and a policy of prices and incomes control or pretended control, the Government has subtly succeeded in transferring to its direct administrative

measures the credit for its fiscal measures. In so far as
it has restrained the cost of living at all, it has done so
by means of these fiscal policies—manipulations of the
bank rate, higher taxation, more rigorous hire purchase
conditions and so on. It has not needed a prices and
incomes policy. It has adopted one for the purpose
of increasing the confidence of foreign bankers and,
most sinister of all, to promote the Socialist aim of
an economy in which the price of everything and
the reward of everybody is settled by central government.

At Exeter on the 29th April, 1967, Powell thus
established his first line of argument—that prices and
incomes policy is totally ineffective:

'Nothing has happened in the last nine months
which had not happened frequently before, when
neither the Prices and Incomes Policy nor Harold
Wilson's government were even dreamt of.

'Take prices first. In the six months of the so-called
freeze, from August 1966 to February 1967, the retail
price index rose 1.1 per cent. "There you are," people
may say, "there's proof for you! The Government's
Prices and Incomes Policy did keep prices down." But
wait. Let us take the trouble to compare what happened
last year with previous years, which anyone can do by
looking at the corresponding figures for the same six
months year by year. The fact is that in no year since
1956—to go no further back—was the increase in that
six months higher than 2 per cent and in fact over the
last eleven years the average increase has been only
1.5 per cent. But there is more to it than that. In 1957–

58 the increase was also just 1.1 per cent; and in 1959–60, supposed to be the period of the "never-had-it-so-good" election boom, the increase was far less—only 0.5 per cent.

'Then take wages. The figures for wages come out slower than those for prices—the latest only cover the first five months of the freeze—and there is no continuous monthly series over a long period of years, as there is for prices. However, from 1963 we have the figures of average earnings in manufacturing and a number of other industries, month by month. These show that in the five months July to December there was a fall not only last year, but in two of the three years before that. No doubt if the series had been started earlier we should find that this is quite a normal pattern in that part of the year. Before 1963 we have got figures for each April and October. Even so, on no fewer than three occasions in seven years there was a rise of only one point in the six-month period—in 1956–57, in 1957–58, and in 1962.

'If the Prices and Incomes Act and all the rest were having any effect, we surely ought to find, especially in the period of the so-called freeze itself, a new pattern altogether, something different in kind from what went before.

'But there is nothing new, nothing unique about what has happened. Whatever caused prices and incomes to behave as they have been doing in the past few months is a cause which was operating long before to produce the same effects on previous occasions.'

As Powell had put it still more vividly at Cottingham on April 21st: 'There is exactly as much evidence to show that the Government's new policies have affected incomes and prices as there is to show that they have affected the weather. It would be no more superstitious to attribute to them the mild and sunny first quarter of this year. The refutation is the same in both cases. It all happened before, when there was no Labour Government, no freeze and no Incomes and Prices Act.'

Powell, however, plainly does not regard the Prices and Incomes Policy simply as an instance of innocent ineffectualness. The second stage in his argument, which he has pursued in innumerable speeches, is concerned to establish in effect that it is impossible efficiently to control the price of anything, or at any rate to secure the general economic advantages of doing so, unless you control the price of everything else. Logically and practically, the Government, he maintains, will be driven to this indefinite extension of its powers.

The Prices and Incomes Policy, in short, embodies the most radical of all socialist aims—an aim so radical that in the past most socialists have always been concerned to repudiate it—the determination by the State of what everyone's income shall be, of what everyone shall pay for everything and therefore ultimately of what everyone shall produce and consume. Characteristically, he alleges, this sinister policy has been introduced in the guise of a non-party expedient to meet a grave national crisis and, characteristically, it has been foisted on the public (already twice) as a temporary expedient.

If the State is to undertake responsibility for the distribution of the entire national income, whatever agency it may employ for the purpose, it must set up criteria of distributive justice or at any rate of economic expediency or of a subtly devised combination of both.

The discovery of these objective criteria is notoriously impossible—from which, incidentally, arises one of the fatal defects of the Marxist theory of value. Who is to say what the objective, monetary worth of any service is? What are the proper standards for deciding pay—the amount of work computed in man-hours involved in production, the results produced during the period of labour, the length of time during which the labourer has occupied his job or some complex calculation of his social needs compared with the social needs of everybody else?

In practice, the standard on which the Government and Mr. Aubrey Jones have relied most has been the least defensible of all—productivity. It is true, of course, that the total national productivity should determine the national total of wages if inflation is to be avoided, but this truism affords no clue at all to the way in which wages should be allotted as between different producers. Apply the principle of productivity to that calculation, and sheer fantasy results.

To begin with, there is no intrinsic economic merit in producing more of any particular commodity. To step up the production of tallow candles when most people want electricity is an instance of economic retrogression. In the second place, Powell would no doubt argue that increased productivity in any industry is most often the result not of additional effort or skill on the part of the workers but of improved technology.

K

In itself, therefore, it constitutes no necessary moral or economic case for higher wages.

The Government has also spoken of simpler and more moving criteria, such as the need to improve the condition of the lowest-paid workers. It has thereby been driven to embark, to Powell's infinite amusement, on the gruelling task of defining what a lowest-paid worker is. The fatuity of this exercise, he predicts, will neither deter the bureaucrats from engaging in it nor prevent them from acting on the arbitrary conclusions which it yields. All that will happen as a consequence is that yet another completely fortuitous consideration, fundamentally political in character, will be introduced to obscure the true function of the wage structure.

That function, it is true, has in part been recognised. In making its recommendations on whether or not wage claims should be satisfied, the Prices and Incomes Board is supposed to take into account the labour requirements of undermanned industries. In other words, it is supposed, so to speak, to re-institute the law of supply and demand. The difference is that a labour shortage, instead of being automatically registered in a rise of wages, must be officially identified and expressed by the bureaucrats. They are fallible in a way in which the law of supply and demand is not. Why employ them to do what, according to Powell, providence has already done for us?

Powell's case against the Prices and Incomes Policy is, thus, an important part of his economic philosophy. This fact distinguishes him from the majority of his ex-colleagues in the Shadow Cabinet. They have been reluctant to abandon wholly and irrevocably the idea of an official intervention in the level of wages. Only by slow degrees have they come round to a decisive rejection of the use of compulsory powers for this purpose. It is still open to them, if they get back to power, to recommend some kind of voluntary attempt at a national wages policy. Powell would have nothing to do with any such compromise: a voluntary wages policy might be more acceptable to him merely on the grounds that it would be less damagingly effective—that, in fact, nobody would take any notice of it.

Powell's conviction is not merely that it will be difficult to enforce wage control; he also believes that it is possibly immoral for either unions or management to accept any other indication of what wages should be than that which is provided by the free market. This is an instance of the depth of difference between Powell and what used to be called 'the great soft centre' of Conservatism. In that he believes that wages should be allowed to find their natural level after a process of free bargaining, his position does not differ from that of Cousins and many of the extreme left of the Labour Party. In a context which has nothing to do with immigration, he may genuinely be described as 'the dockers' friend'.

What prevents the majority of his colleagues from agreeing with him and from thereby exploiting one of the inherent weaknesses of the Labour Party—its commitment to socialism and its dependence on free trade unions—is a spectre which has haunted every British government since the war. It is the feeling that, in conditions of relatively full employment, a powerful trade-union movement, fortified by legal privileges and able, through the operation of the closed shop, to intensify labour shortage, will be in a position to dictate to the community.

What will happen, for instance, if the railwaymen suddenly threaten to withdraw an essential national service unless they receive an uneconomic increase in pay? Will the Government not be forced either to yield to this demand, thereby putting up the price of all goods which depend on the railways for their distribution, or to deny it, thereby ruining the export trade? Powell seems to be asking the government to forswear the right even to urge workers to restrain their avarice in such circumstances. To understand his reply to this criticism it is necessary to understand his views on the trade unions.

Powell's views on the trade-union movement represent one of the most independent and widely misunderstood elements of his thought. He begins by challenging the whole concept of the trade union as an economic institution. The view that it came into being as a calculated device for securing a higher reward for workers than would be available in the free market is, he maintains, not borne out by the facts. If that was the intention (so he argued in a famous paper to the Manchester Statistical Society), it has conspicuously failed. On the whole, wages have risen somewhat more rapidly in industries, such as domestic service, which have not been covered by trade unions than in those which have. The most, it would seem, that can rationally be claimed for the union movement is that it has had an indirect effect in stimulating wage rises in those sectors of economic life with which it has not meddled.

In Powell's view, the utter failure of the unions to achieve the object for which they are supposed to exist is not hard to explain. The method by which they are pursuing that object is foredoomed to failure. It consists, in practice, of an attempt to distort the labour market by producing an artificial shortage of workers.

The collective refusal of workers to work within a given industry unless they all receive a payment for their services greater than that which most of them could exact if they were in competition with each other can do nothing, even in the medium-length view, to promote the interests of the working classes. There must in practice be a limit to the amount of money which an industry can afford to dispense in wages. If existing workers in that industry demand rewards which are in excess of that limit, all of them plainly cannot be satisfied. If some are satisfied, it must be at the expense of reducing the labour force by dismissing others. Conversely, if a union insists that none of its members shall in any circumstances be dismissed by the management—if it insists, that is to say, on maintaining in full employment more workers than the industry needs—this can be done only at the cost of depressing the remuneration of the average worker.

Of course, a government which is prepared to finance all wage increases by inflation may temporarily obscure these facts, but the illusion will be short-lived. The increased wages will soon be cancelled out by increased prices. Of course, also, wage demands may be satisfied by means of asking a higher price for the commodity produced, but here again the effect will be short-lived and illusory. Demand for the commodity will decline as the price grows greater, and again the result must be unemployment or the depression of wages.

To the old socialist contention that increased wages can be supplied out of diminished shareholders' profits, Powell would no doubt reply that there are strict limits within which such encroachment can be made without rendering investment so unprofitable as to lead to its withdrawal.

The basis of Powell's argument, therefore, is that the trade unions are literally powerless to alter the operation of the law of supply and demand to their own advantage. His reasoning on this point is well illustrated by an extract from a speech delivered in Birmingham on the 1st December, 1967:

'The public are appalled by the current railway dispute. They are not so much appalled by the inhospitality of the drivers and footplatemen who begrudge the guard a nice comfortable seat on the engine doing nothing. They are appalled by the revelation, or the reminder, that the N.U.R. and British Railways had agreed that where there is no guard's van on a train and no function for a guard, the guards should nevertheless be paid to ride on the engine doing nothing.

'These men are riding at the public's expense, because their pay for doing nothing is one of the elements in the railways' annual deficit of £150 million which is footed by the taxpayer. But there is something which distresses me a great deal more. The guards are in reality travelling at their own expense because it is the overmanning of the railways, on which their union and the management have agreed, that keeps their pay and that of other railwaymen so low.

'The victims of all restrictive and inefficient practices are the workers themselves. Here is a classic instance where, as things stand, the objects of the trade unions are in direct opposition to the interests of their own members. The railwaymen are low-paid. They are always complaining their wages lag behind the general movement of wages. They are right. But why is it so? It is because their unions, aided and abetted by the management which is in cahoots with them, and by the politicians who are afraid of them, have organised and preserved a colossal waste of manpower in the railways. The result, automatically and inevitably, is that the manpower is low paid.

'The unions do not care, because the interest of their organisers is to have the maximum number of members to contribute to their own importance. The management and the politicians do not care, because they can make the taxpayer pay up to avoid a row. It is the men that suffer. The Labour Party will not speak for them. The unions will not speak for them. The only party which speaks for them is the party not afraid to attack restriction, monopoly and waste of manpower wherever they are found.'

Powell, in fact, regards the trade unions as social institutions into whose myth there has been built a profound economic fallacy. Nevertheless, they exist, and must be fitted into the framework of the law. Genuinely free and voluntary organisations are an important element in the structure of a society, and it is not unreasonable to speak of rights appertaining to them. Powell does not regard himself as an anti-trade unionist. On the contrary, he thinks of the Government and the leaders of the T.U.C. as arch examples of anti-trade unionism.

He sees in the T.U.C.'s policy of voluntary restraint and in the close collaboration between it, the Confederation of British Industries and the Government the seeds of the corporate state. He makes the point in a speech given at the South Oxfordshire Conservative Political Conference on the 11th March, 1967.

' "Don't you worry," says the T.U.C. and the C.B.I. to the Government, "to concern yourself with details. We will undertake to manage our own side of the show, and deliver the goods." Listen to this from the Prime Minister, when announcing—though not to the House of Commons—the Government's intention to maintain compulsory powers:

' "Each year government and industry will sit down together with all the figures and forecasts available to us. We then discuss together an assessment of what, in relation to production and the calls upon that production, the national dividend can be for the year ahead. A national dividend for distribution between all forms of income, for distribution to workers by hand and by brain. It will then be for the trade union movement, through the machinery it is developing, to

form its own judgments as to priorities and timing, but
to form them on a basis which ensures that the amount
distributed in higher pay does not run ahead of the
amount we earn by our production. This will be a
new concept, unique in a democracy (note that) in this
or any other country, and I pay my tribute in saying
that it was the events of yesterday which made it
possible."

'I will come in a moment to the meeting of the
T.U.C. to which he was referring, and I am not here
chiefly concerned with the fact that the whole system
described is economic poppycock. I will on that score
just mention two points. First, that official estimates
of the future national production are usually wildly
wrong—see the late unlamented National Plan—and
so would make nonsense of any scheme based on them.
Secondly, even if one could know the "national dividend" in advance, the task of dividing it up amongst
all the shareholders is far beyond the resources of any
organisation except by proceeding on brutally crass
rules-of-thumb.

'However, what I am concerned with here is the
function in this scheme which the T.U.C. is to per-
form. To it is to be delegated the detailed work of
distribution, what the Prime Minister called "the
priorities and timing"—in other words, what money
actual people are actually to be allowed to get. Believe
it or not, this function was actually accepted for the
T.U.C. by a huge majority of their card vote at the
Central Hall last week.

'It is not in any ordinary sense of the word a voluntary scheme which the T.U.C. was thus given authority

by its members to implement. The word "voluntary" is a snare and a delusion in this context. Listen to what Mr George Woodcock said on that occasion. "Sooner or later, some lad will go ahead whatever the law may say. What are the Government going to do then? Are they going to send all the recalcitrants to prison? That is the implication of legislation." I dare say a lot of people, including a lot of trade unionists and other workers when they read or heard those words, thought "Good; quite right; he is against compulsion." But is he? Read on! "If anybody can deal with recalcitrants," continued Woodcock, "it is us"; and, to leave no doubt about it, he added:

' "This is a tough business. It is a damned unpleasant business, and the only justification would be that it is accepted as a normal part of trade unionism."

'Now, who are these "recalcitrants" who are going to be "dealt with" by the T.U.C? The Prime Minister had a word to say to them at the same question time this week. He called them "minorities who seek their own selfish interests". This is how all oppressors smear their intended victims. Translate, then, while you are still allowed to do so, into ordinary English. It means "workers, whether in unions or not, who get the best available price for their labour, when that price does not happen to be the one approved by the T.U.C. or Harold Wilson".

'I had occasion last week publicly to expose some of the methods by which a union was "dealing" with such recalcitrants, namely with employed draughtsmen who did not choose to join the union and with draughtsmen who were hiring out their services on their own account. The method was to use the power of the union, acting through the employers, to force the unwilling workers (known to the Prime Minister as a "selfish minority") to join the union. How right George Woodcock was when he said that his trade unions were "used to dealing with recalcitrants".'

Powell's fire is directed mainly, therefore, against the current policy of maintaining and where necessary restoring the legal privileges of the unions merely in order to transform the unions into more serviceable instruments of government. His own policy is the complete reverse of this: he would weaken the degree of authority exerted by the unions over their members, while at the same time abandoning the attempt to subject these organisations to government control. He would abolish the closed shop and attack all restrictive and conspiratorial practices; but he would also sweep away wages policy.

Plainly, Powell's ideal world would be one in which workers competed with each other as individuals and the price of labour was fixed exclusively by the force of the market. He has never gone so far, however, as to condemn collective bargaining. He realises that this is an institution which has come to stay and is prepared to tolerate the restrictive elements within it provided they do not assume what he would regard as a grotesque and damaging form, the form which they assume at present and which arises fundamentally from the institution of the closed shop.

He does not wish to see trade unions given a defined

status and function within a national economic system; he wishes them to be treated as private associations within the limits of the law and he wishes the law to be so constructed as to show a scrupulous regard for the rights of members of these associations as individuals. He is plainly sceptical of, though he has not repudiated outright, the declared policy of his party on the future of the unions. He believes it to make too many concessions to the corporatist idea, which he holds to be one ingredient in contemporary British political thought which can be accurately described as 'fascist'. If, for instance, the Tory policy of making unions responsible for the fulfilment of the contracts they make on behalf of their members were to be adopted, would it not follow that the government was really appealing to union leaders to discipline their members on its behalf? Would not the formula really be 'we (the State) make our agreement with you, you see that your men carry it out'? Fundamentally, Powell believes that the only real contracts are between individuals.

It is obvious that, like much of the rest of his economic gospel, Powell's teaching on the trade unions has a rigorous mathematical quality about it which nevertheless leaves many assumptions untested. It is another example of his almost naive interpretation of classical liberalism. Powell is persuaded (and justly so) that the use of trade unions to bring about an artificial increase in the prosperity of their members is foredoomed to failure. All other considerations apart, when workers organise for this purpose they call into existence parallel organisations of employers to resist it, and the competitive influence of the one kind of combination is, at least in some degree, counteracted by that of the other.

Nevertheless, the conviction remains that this is what trade unions are for and the myth survives that it is their existence which is primarily responsible for the vast increase in the welfare of workers during the last half-century. Men will continue to act on this myth. (In all other spheres, at any rate, Powell is healthily sceptical of the practicability of educating prejudices out of existence.) In the process of acting on it, they may do themselves little ultimate good, but they can do the community infinite harm. Has the state no ultimate right to control their behaviour or even to seek, by supplying them with relevant information, to induce them to pursue their interests in an enlightened way consistent with the well-being of society?

As usual, Powell gives the impression of being unwilling to admit these ultimate rights for fear of the danger which must follow of their being pressed to extreme lengths. It is possible to admit them without dissenting from his view that the elaborate and detailed control of wages either by the T.U.C. or the government is at best a fatuous and in its full development a disastrous policy. His own arguments, which have already had a beneficent influence on his party, might have had still greater influence had he resisted the temptation to squeeze more out of them than they yield. Had Powell confined himself to emphasising the appalling dangers inherent in the attempt to extend state intervention to the suppression of free collective bargaining he would have been on stronger ground.

What may be disposed of emphatically, however, is the calumny that he favours the smashing of trade unionism. He would plainly like to see the bargaining power of the unions kept as far as possible within the limits of economic realities. He would not tolerate the smallest infringement of their freedom as lawful voluntary associations.

Powell's image as the hard-faced bank manager has led to considerable misunderstandings about his views on the welfare state, misunderstandings which have persisted, among friends and enemies alike, in spite of his record when at the Ministry of Health. The popular view is still, probably, that if he headed a government he would embark on a systematic process of demolishing the welfare state and of substituting for flat rate benefits and contributions a rigorous and not particularly generous system of means tested provision against, but only against, the major catastrophes of life.

The seed of truth in this idea is Powell's permanent and unshakeable conviction that the limits to the possible expansion of welfare in all fields are set by the nation's wealth and the limits of State-provided welfare are set by the taxable capacity of the community. He has more than once turned with fury against the easy assumption that national wealth can actually be increased by greater expenditure on social services.

While energetically spending at the Ministry of Health, he constantly attacked the view that the case for this spending was that it would lead to an increase in national productivity. More recently, he has applied his lash with equal vigour to the same doctrine in respect of education. As usual, he has not been content to make the obvious and incontestible point—that there is no necessary correlation between increased spending in these areas and increased national income. He has at least seemed to imply that there are absolutely no circumstances in which increased spending on schools and doctors can possibly contribute, as one factor among many, to greater industrial production.

The defect is small compared with the crucial character of the truth he is conveying. Successive governments have all been helped in their determination to plan their social expenditure on the basis of absurdly inflated ideas about national growth by the illusion that this expenditure was itself a direct and powerful agent of growth—that every new technician produced by the universities could instantly be classified as a measurable economic asset.

National production must determine national expenditure. Yet Powell has held with equal consistency from the beginning of his political career that it is the business of government to secure a minimum standard of life below which no one should fall. This view he has sharply distinguished from the conceptions favoured by socialists that it is the business of government to supply the citizen with all the material essentials of the good life and that these essentials shall be free at the point of consumption.

Nevertheless, this distinction has never led him to reject hook, line and sinker the whole apparatus of the

Beveridge welfare system. He was one of the first to point out the limitations of the national insurance principle and its essentially fictitious character. Since compulsory insurance contributions pay for only a minute proportion of the benefits to which they give access, the State is obliged to supply the difference out of taxation, much of which is progressive in its incidence—that is to say hits the rich and the relatively rich disproportionately hard. Wherever taxation is invoked to supplement insurance provisions, there is, in principle, a case for applying some kind of means test to the distribution of benefits. However, where, as is broadly true in the case of the health service, an equal benefit is conferred upon all, the principle of help according to need is still, up to a point, preserved by the very fact of progressive taxation. All men receive the same service, but each contributes to its total cost according to his capacity.

It is not only on grounds of administrative convenience that this arrangement may prove preferable to a system which rests on charging different prices for the same service to different people. Powell is aware of the menacing egalitarian potentialities of the principle of selectivity now so fashionable in all political parties. It could, in practice mean, for instance, an oppressive form of double taxation of the middle classes required to contribute disproportionately to the cost of building schools and paying doctors and to pay again disproportionately for the cost of using them. He is conscious like the rest of his Party of the deterrent effects of heavy taxation progressively imposed. Even the substantial switch to indirect taxation favoured by his Party could not go so far as to wipe out these effects altogether. It seems likely, therefore, that Powell would maintain substantial areas of the welfare state fundamentally as they are now.

In other areas, principally concerned with the dispensing of actual monetary payments, he would favour an enquiry into means. While still in the Macmillan administration, he prepared in collaboration with Iain Macleod proposals for the reform of the system of retirement pensions, proposals which his Party has never accepted and which it is today further from accepting than ever before.

They provided for a generous guaranteed minimum State retirement pension. In other words, on retirement, a man's resources would be investigated and the government would supplement them to the extent required to assure him of a decent level of subsistence. The minds of all political parties are now firmly set in the opposite direction—that is to say, in the direction of a comprehensive system of graduated pensions based on the level of earnings and financed by graduated contributions similarly based. To Powell, these tendencies are abhorrent. The function of State policy towards the aged is to achieve reasonable redistribution, not to impose the duty of providence. If a man wishes to spend when he is young at the cost of his comfort when he is old it is not the business of politicians to stop him, though they may mitigate the consequences of his folly.

Powell was in the vanguard of those who attacked indiscriminate housing subsidies. Years ago, he was already advocating the gradual transfer of housing

L

expenditure from the local councils to central government and provision of individual housing allowances on proof of need. He anticipated much of what is now official Conservative policy and some of the ideas which are now specifically associated with Sir Keith Joseph.

On health, Powell has continued to point out the inherent defects of a universal service which is free at the point of consumption. He has shrunk, however, from suggesting that this characteristic can be altered. His attitude, on this point, still seems to be that expressed in the celebrated maxim—we live in the best possible of all worlds and everything in it is a necessary evil.

On education, Powell is considerably nearer to the official position of his party than many of its critics. It is true that he has eloquently though abstractly defended the view that educational selection is essential. He opposes the drift towards comprehensivisation, though he has so far been less than explicit on the extent to which he would go in pressing his view in defiance of local councils. Though critical of the assumption that all expenditure on university education is valuable (and violently critical of the heresy that such expenditure is specifically valuable as an element in economic growth), he has never subscribed to the idea, favoured by many of those who admire his general economic and social thinking, that part of the cost should be met out of loans to undergraduates repayable when they begin to earn.

Powell pays eloquent tribute to the view that those who receive public welfare should be given the widest possible measure of choice about the form which it should take, but his concessions to this view have not so far been substantial. He will have no truck, for example, with the proposal for educational vouchers— the idea that government should finance its contribution to education by vouchers which parents could use at their discretion in the State or private schools and which they could supplement if they so wished out of their own incomes.

No doubt the distrust which this proposal inspires in Powell is due largely to the fact that it would involve a considerable immediate increase in public expenditure—the same objection, in fact, as he raised against the proposal for free prescriptions for private health patients. It is also due largely to his fear that the State educational system might be grievously damaged if the method of financing it were altered in this way. Powell is emphatically a friend of that system and would prefer the State to concentrate on improving it rather than to be diverted by the desire either to bolster up or destroy the independent sector.

If Powell were in control of the government, the welfare state would be reformed in some respects drastically, but the reform would be piecemeal. He would hope indeed that in course of time and with increasing prosperity more and more people would make private provision for their own needs by voluntary insurance, thereby safeguarding and extending their sphere of choice. There is little evidence that he would do much directly by State action to promote this process or that he would depart from his own consistently held lifetime belief in the 'basic minimum'. The moderation of his ideas in this field, if understood, would disappoint many of his admirers and confound many of his critics.

The lynch-pin of Powell's economic philosophy is his advocacy of the floating pound. Of all the fallacies afflicting government in recent years, he finds none more dangerous than that it is possible advantageously to alter the true market relationship at any given moment between the value of sterling and that of foreign currencies.

This, he argues, is an area in which illusion cannot be preserved for long. Government in the end must yield to facts by altering the fixed rate of exchange to meet changing realities. Powell is at present convinced that the latest devaluation has done precisely this; if realities change adversely or favourably, however, the fixed exchange rates will eventually have to follow them. A floating pound, he contends, will bring this adjustment about automatically and without the political upheavals attendant on devaluation, which it is the natural instinct of political parties to resist too long.

The merits of the floating pound are the subject of heated and highly technical discussion between economists. Against Powell the view is strongly urged that a floating pound would expose the economy even more seriously than it already is exposed to the vicissitudes of financial speculation and that the fixed exchange, though it must not be allowed to attempt too strident or too prolonged a defiance of the facts, does supply a stabilising factor.

What matters essentially, however, is Powell's commitment to the view that the first duty of the government in its handling of economics is to ensure that the exchange rate shall be realistic. Its second duty he sees as being the rigorous maintenance at home of a balance between production and the monetary resources available for expenditure. No daydreams of welfare or national grandeur should be allowed to distract statesmen from this elementary task of book-keeping.

For the rest, Powell, in theory at least, would confine State activity to the regulation of the economy in the strict meaning of that term—to the imposition of general laws applying to the community at large and designed principally to frustrate attempts at arbitrary interference with the operation of supply and demand. He emphatically repudiates the view that an economy thus organised must depend on a substantial and continuing measure of unemployment. There is no reason why the balance between production and monetary resources should not have the effect of producing a high and reasonably stable level of employment.

Powell would embark on a systematic plan for extending the area of private enterprise at the cost of the public sector. He would not shrink from denationalising and he has considerable confidence in the capacity of the City to arrange the private finance needed for such an operation. He would ruthlessly sweep away as many as possible of the official and semiofficial bodies which try to unite government and industry in the direction, by ostensibly voluntary means, of national economic activity. He would probably fail to find any constructive occupation for the National Prices and Incomes Board.

Here, as elsewhere, what Powell would do would in practice be determined by his sense of what was politically possible, a sense which has often proved shrewd and may sometimes be thought to have erred on the side of timidity. Yet the general outlines of his policy are clear, and they sharply distinguish him from those of his Conservative colleagues who are still bound by the concepts of the Macmillan era, still think in terms of 'indicative planning' and still flirt uncertainly with the idea of a National Incomes Policy. He presents his Party, in fact, with a real choice, a choice which is nonetheless real for being often defined in too rigid and abstract terms.

As an economic programme, Powellism, even allowing for its author's capacity to adapt to political circumstances, will remain thoroughly radical. It appeals strongly to various sentiments which are currently under-represented in politics and in particular in the Tory Party—middle class ire at high taxation and the bureaucratic planning which it expensively sustains and working class opposition to encroachments on trade union freedom. Powell's political hope is plainly that the working class distaste for these encroachments may eventually prove a stronger factor than the attractions of a broadly egalitarian policy to the proletarian mind. He is seeking a drastic re-alignment of social forces in politics—comparable perhaps with the early Disraelian dream of a coalition between urban working men and the Tory squirearchy.

Inevitably, in such a coalition, both sides would have to sacrifice something. In this connection, the relative moderation of Powell's views on the welfare state is of importance. Those views, for instance, grievously disappoint such fervent and accomplished evangelists for selectivity and choice as the Institute of Economic Affairs, a body which is otherwise disposed to deep reverence for Powell. Apparently doctrinaire as Powell's approach to economics is, it has evidently not been formulated with a high-minded disregard for long-term calculations of political advantage.

VII

Conclusions

OF the popular illusions about Enoch Powell which this essay has set out to challenge, none is more obstinate than the notion that he is primarily an intellectual and only secondarily a politician. The reverse is almost true. He has, indeed, a greater volume and variety of knowledge than most other politicians and a capacity for sustained reasoning which distinguishes him from most though not all of his colleagues in the Conservative Party. The belief that he is logically infallible, however, is wide of the mark. The package in which his often complex thoughts are presented is so impressive that the faculties of his critics are sometimes paralysed by the mere contemplation of it. Look at his arguments more deeply and they often reveal tacit and highly contentious assumptions and inferences too easily drawn. He will sometimes be found (and his famous speech on immigration was a case in point) to be subordinating logical rigour to the demands of style, a fault not uncommon in classical scholars who readily equate the balanced period with the indestructible argument.

Certainly the attribution of political innocence which usually accompanies this reputation for intellectual purity is, in Powell's case, even further from the truth. There are some kinds of political activity at which he is not adept. He does not flourish in close oligarchies; he is not skilled at making subtle personal alliances; he lacks the humility or subtleness necessary to successful intrigue. His code of political loyalty is rigidly reasoned out and strictly observed, but it does not include some of the woollier conventions of camaraderie which are important to his colleagues. Though not cold, he is detached to the extent that his principles are thought out in advance of being stated and are not easily modified by contact with the opinion of others. His contribution to the work of any team, therefore, is bound to be strongly distinctive.

It is this fact, no doubt, which explains why in some quarters he has recently acquired another kind of reputation which is almost fantastically false, that of being some sort of fascist or semi-fascist demagogue who is appealing over the heads of the political establishment to the prejudice and violence of the mob.

A more ludicrous distortion is hard to imagine. Powell is by nature a parliamentarian. By conviction, he is at least as much of a Whig as of a Tory. He is by instinct as well as doctrine a libertarian, sometimes to the point of fanaticism. He believes, as a good Whig should, in political hierarchy. He has been less inclined than many of his colleagues to enlist popular passions in support of his opinions or his ambitions. The kind of activity in which Mr. Quintin Hogg indulged, for example, at the Conservative Party Conference of 1963 (the occasion, it will be recalled, on which he 'sacrificed' a peerage for the service of his country) would not come easily to him.

In the accusation of demagogy, there is this much and only this much truth: Powell, like many others, has observed the increasing gulf which is developing between the politicians on both sides and the mass of the electorate. He has tried, on one crucial issue, to bridge it.

In selecting, consciously or otherwise, immigration as the point at which the bridge was to be built, he was, up to a point, merely reflecting the views of his own constituents. Yet, there was plainly more in it than that: his speech came at the climax of a campaign mainly dedicated to winning public support for carefully reasoned economic doctrines which, as stated by Powell, had little emotive appeal. The people may be tired of bureaucrats and oppressed by taxation, but the law of supply and demand does not seem to them to be pure poetry nor capitalism a 'gift of the Holy Ghost'.

Like other politicians, Powell has achieved the strongest response when giving vent to one of the less important though wholly sincere of his convictions. There are dangers in this, but they do not justify the charge that he has whipped up racial hatred for the sake of political advantage. The most that may be fairly said on that point is that his mind may have been running on the lines indicated in this possibly prophetic passage of an essay by Mr. John Biffen published three years ago:

There is no tangible evidence of the effect of coloured immigration on the voting habits of the electorate but it is possible that Tory attitudes on immigration will strike a working-class response and replace the old-style imperialism that traditionally attracted, say, the Lancashire working-class to the idea of Tory democracy.*

The analogy which this suggests between Joseph Chamberlain and Powell is, I believe, helpful to an understanding of Powell's position in politics today. Chamberlain's mission was to convert the Conservative Party to a doctrine and a policy—to imperialism and to a vigorous and radical concern for social reform. Powell also conceives himself to have a mission of no less dramatic a kind—the conversion of the Conservative Party from an outmoded imperialism to a realistic patriotism and from a largely dirigist and paternalistic view of economic policy to a radical policy of economic liberalism. Chamberlain sought and Powell is seeking to alter the nature of the Conservative Party—to transform it from a 'safe' party, to be turned to for sound administration in a crisis—into a positive and dynamic party with a defined political and social faith.

Such transformations are not congenial to the spirit of Conservatism. Chamberlain never became leader of the Tories. In a supreme national crisis he might have done, and so might Powell. Certainly, the view that Powell's principles are so rigid that he could never achieve the capacity for compromise indispensable to the effective leadership of the party is not borne out by his career. His lust for political and administrative

---

* *The Conservative Opportunity.* Published June, 1965. Batsford in conjunction with the Conservative Political Centre. 18s.

activity is at least as strong as his intellectual consistency. The probability must remain, however, that
Powell will not lead the Tories, a probability which he
would certainly admit himself and which I suspect
causes him no special anguish.

The task of containing Chamberlainite imperialism
within the Conservative Party was a main pre-occupation of Tory statesmanship during much of the
inter-war period. It was often a great source of weakness
and division in the party. Chamberlain, it is true, was
an adept party manager; Powell is not. Yet, it is un-
deniable that Powell appeals as Chamberlain did to
powerful popular sentiments which the Tory leadership will neglect at its peril.

What is more, 'Powellism', like Chamberlainite
imperialism, offers the Tory Party a rare chance to
achieve a permanent and solid foothold in areas of
society which are assumed to belong by right to its
opponents—in other words, among the working classes.
One measure of a politician's skill is his ability to
gather together in a single package a miscellany of
popular ambitions and grievances which left to themselves conflict with each other. Powell offers the middle
classes a free economy; he offers working class opinion
not only or primarily resistance to immigration but
also resistance to incomes policy; he thereby effectively
exploits the central weakness of Labour—the tension
between its philosophy of state control and its dependence on the trade unions. One may even add to this list
Powell's advocacy of a foreign policy more independent of the U.S.A. and his zeal for the reduction of
foreign commitments. In these respects, his pro-

gramme might in practice be more congenial to many a leftist than is that of Harold Wilson. Like the young Disraeli, Powell is attempting nothing less than a drastic political re-alignment of the classes, a new version of Tory democracy.

This is something more and something less than a challenge to the leadership of Heath. Powell has been and remains scrupulously determined not to be involved in plans for a palace revolution in the Conservative Party. He has bigger fish to fry than that. He is challenging not the Leader, but the Party's fundamental habits of thought.

What has given the impression of a challenge to Heath is the intrinsic weakness of the Conservative leadership at present That weakness is not due solely to Heath's limitations. The Tory Party has not yet recovered from the effect of two leadership crises which rapidly followed each other. It has not even recovered from the transformation of the whole concept of the leader which came about as the result of the adoption of an elective system.

It is, and it ought to be, profoundly disturbed by the evidence that its leader continues to be widely unpopular in the country at a time when its fortunes are so dramatically improving (evidence, surely, that it is benefiting chiefly from disillusion with Labour). At the same time, it is wholly conscious of the dangers of any attempt to change the leadership yet again in the absence of any acceptable alternative to Heath.

This last fact confers considerable strength on the leader, but it is a strength which at any moment may disappear. His task, like that of all Party leaders, is to

hold a coalition together. For that, there is much in
Heath's make-up to commend him. As a Chief Whip,
he had the reputation of being as gentle as a dove and
as wise as a serpent. He used at least to be gifted
with the capacity for compromise. He is an empiricist
unencumbered by rigid doctrines, a man who might be
expected successfully to hold the balance between
opposing views.

Yet, it is precisely this that, on a large variety of
issues, he has failed to do. The rigid discipline which he
has sought (though often conspicuously failed) to impose on his Shadow Cabinet is not fitting to a Party in
Opposition. He has helped to stultify the process of
re-definition which his Party has urgently needed from
1963 onwards. He is suspected increasingly of depend-
ing on the counsel of a few congenial men who in turn
are suspected by large sections of the Party of being
outmoded relics of the Macmillanite conception of progressive Toryism.

Those suspicions were strengthened by Heath's
recent decision not to oppose the Race Relations Bill
on its Third Reading in spite of having opposed it by
a reasoned amendment on its Second Reading. The
importance of that issue and of the rebellion in the
Tory Party to which it led were both exaggerated by
the Press. Nevertheless, Tory discontent with the
leader on this occasion was due in part to the feeling
that Shadow Cabinet policy had suffered in clarity and
constancy from Powell's dismissal. That feeling may
well grow dangerously in the months that lie ahead.

The strength of Powell's position, however, does
not, it must be insisted, arise from any capacity or

inclination on his part for intrigue at Westminster. It consists precisely in the strength of his ideas. They offer the Conservatives a unique opportunity for positively restating their philosophy and appealing to feelings in the country which in the long run cannot be ignored with impunity.

Containing Powellism, if not Powell, will, I believe, be the main pre-occupation of Tory internal politics for the next decade at least. By impetuously dismissing Powell from the Shadow Cabinet (though the action was not unprovoked), Heath has for the moment declined that task. That was a serious mistake.

Is it irreparable?

Speech by The Rt. Hon. J. Enoch Powell, M.P. to the Annual General Meeting of the West Midlands Area Conservative Political Centre at the Midland Hotel, Birmingham, 2.30 p.m. Saturday, 20th April, 1968.

M

THE supreme function of statesmanship is to provide against preventable evils. In seeking to do so, it encounters obstacles which are deeply rooted in human nature. One is that by the very order of things such evils are not demonstrable until they have occurred: at each stage in their onset there is room for doubt and for dispute whether they be real or imaginary. By the same token, they attract little attention in comparison with current troubles, which are both indisputable and pressing: whence the besetting temptation of all politics to concern itself with the immediate present at the expense of the future. Above all, people are disposed to mistake predicting troubles for causing troubles and even for desiring troubles: 'if only', they love to think, 'if only people wouldn't talk about it, it probably wouldn't happen'. Perhaps this habit goes back to the primitive belief that the word and the thing, the name and the object, are identical. At all events, the discussion of future grave but, with effort now, avoidable evils is the most unpopular and at the same time the most necessary occupation for the politician. Those who knowingly shirk it, deserve, and not infrequently receive, the curses of those who come after.

A week or two ago I fell into conversation with a constituent, a middle-aged, quite ordinary working man employed in one of our nationalised industries.

After a sentence or two about the weather, he suddenly said: 'If I had the money to go, I wouldn't stay in this country.' I made some deprecatory reply, to the effect that even this government wouldn't last for ever; but he took no notice, and continued: 'I have three children, all of them been through grammar school and two of them married now, with family. I shan't be satisfied till I have seen them all settled overseas. In this country in fifteen or twenty years' time the black man will have the whip hand over the white man.'

I can already hear the chorus of execration. How dare I say such a horrible thing? How dare I stir up trouble and inflame feelings by repeating such a conversation? The answer is that I do not have the right not to do so. Here is a decent, ordinary fellow Englishman, who in broad daylight in my own town says to me, his Member of Parliament, that this country will not be worth living in for his children. I simply do not have the right to shrug my shoulders and think about something else. What he is saying, thousands and hundreds of thousands are saying and thinking—not throughout Great Britain, perhaps, but in the areas that are already undergoing the total transformation to which there is no parallel in a thousand years of English history.

In fifteen or twenty years, on present trends, there will be in this country $3\frac{1}{2}$ million Commonwealth immigrants and their descendants. That is not my figure. That is the official figure given to Parliament by the spokesman of the Registrar General's office. There is no comparable official figure for the year

2,000, but it must be in the region of 5–7 million, approximately one-tenth of the whole population, and approaching that of Greater London. Of course, it will not be evenly distributed from Margate to Aberystwyth and from Penzance to Aberdeen. Whole areas, towns and parts of towns across England will be occupied by different sections of the immigrant and immigrant-descended population.

As time goes on, the proportion of this total who are immigrant descendants, those born in England, who arrived here by exactly the same route as the rest of us, will rapidly increase. Already by 1985 the native-born would constitute the majority. It is this fact above all which creates the extreme urgency of action now, of just that kind of action which is hardest for politicians to take, action where the difficulties lie in the present but the evils to be prevented or minimised lie several parliaments ahead.

The natural and rational first question with a nation confronted by such a prospect is to ask: 'how can its dimensions be reduced?' Granted it be not wholly preventable, can it be limited, bearing in mind that numbers are of the essence: the significance and consequences of an alien element introduced into a country or population are profoundly different according to whether that element is one per cent or ten per cent. The answers to the simple and rational question are equally simple and rational: by stopping, or virtually stopping, further inflow, and by promoting the maximum outflow. Both answers are part of the official policy of the Conservative Party.

It almost passes belief that at this moment twenty or

thirty additional immigrant children are arriving from overseas in Wolverhampton alone every week—and that means fifteen or twenty additional families of a decade or two hence. Those whom the gods wish to destroy, they first make mad. We must be mad, literally mad, as a nation to be permitting the annual inflow of some 50,000 dependents, who are for the most part the material of the future growth of the immigrant-descended population. It is like watching a nation busily engaged in heaping up its own funeral pyre. So insane are we that we actually permit unmarried persons to immigrate for the purpose of founding a family with spouses and fiancés whom they have never seen. Let no-one suppose that the flow of dependents will automatically tail off. On the contrary, even at the present admission rate of only 5,000 a year by voucher, there is sufficient for a further 25,000 dependents per annum ad infinitum, without taking into account the huge reservoir of existing relations in this country—and I am making no allowance at all for fraudulent entry. In these circumstances nothing will suffice but that the total inflow for settlement should be reduced at once to negligible proportions, and that the necessary legislative and administrative measures be taken without delay. I stress the words 'for settlement'. This has nothing to do with the entry of Commonwealth citizens, any more than of aliens, into this country, for the purposes of study or of improving their qualifications, like (for instance) the Commonwealth doctors who, to the advantage of their own countries, have enabled our hospital service to be expanded faster than would otherwise have been possible. These are not, and never have been, immigrants.

I turn to re-emigration. If all immigration ended tomorrow, the rate of growth of the immigrant and immigrant-descended population would be substantially reduced, but the prospective size of this element in the population would still leave the basic character of the national danger unaffected. This can only be tackled while a considerable proportion of the total still comprises persons who entered this country during the last ten years or so. Hence the urgency of implementing now the second element of the Conservative Party's policy: the encouragement of re-emigration. Nobody can make an estimate of the numbers which, with generous grants and assistance, would choose either to return to their countries of origin or to go to other countries anxious to receive the manpower and the skills they represent. Nobody knows, because no such policy has yet been attempted. I can only say that, even at present, immigrants in my own constituency from time to time come to me, asking if I can find them assistance to return home. If such a policy were adopted and pursued with the determination which the gravity of the alternative justifies, the resultant outflow could appreciably alter the prospects for the future.

It can be no part of any policy that existing families should be kept divided; but there are two directions in which families can be reunited, and if our former and present immigration laws have brought about the division of families, albeit voluntarily or semi-voluntarily, we ought to be prepared to arrange for them to be re-united in their countries of origin. In short, suspension of immigration and encouragement of re-emigration hang together, logically and humanly, as two aspects of the same approach.

The third element of the Conservative Party's policy is that all who are in this country as citizens should be equal before the law and that there shall be no discrimination or difference made between them by public authority. As Mr. Heath has put it, we will have no 'first-class citizens' and 'second-class citizens'. This does not mean that the immigrant and his descendants should be elevated into a privileged or special class or that the citizen should be denied his right to discriminate in the management of his own affairs between one fellow-citizen and another or that he should be subjected to imposition as to his reasons and motives for behaving in one lawful manner rather than another.

There could be no grosser misconception of the realities than is entertained by those who vociferously demand legislation as they call it 'against discrimination', whether they be leader-writers of the same kidney and sometimes on the same newspapers which year after year in the 1930's tried to blind this country to the rising peril which confronted it, or archbishops who live in palaces, faring delicately with the bedclothes pulled right up over their heads. They have got it exactly and diametrically wrong. The discrimination and the deprivation, the sense of alarm and of resentment, lies not with the immigrant population but with those among whom they have come and are still coming. This is why to enact legislation of the kind before Parliament at this moment is to risk throwing a match onto gunpowder. The kindest thing that can be said about those who propose and support it is that they know not what they do.

Nothing is more misleading than comparison between the Commonwealth immigrant in Britain and the American negro. The negro population of the United States, which was already in existence before the United States became a nation started literally as slaves and were later given the franchise and other rights of citizenship, to the exercise of which they have only gradually and still incompletely come. The Commonwealth immigrant came to Britain as a full citizen, to a country which knew no discrimination between one citizen and another, and he entered instantly into the possession of the rights of every citizen, from the vote to free treatment under the National Health Service. Whatever drawbacks attended the immigrants —and they were drawbacks which did not, and do not, make admission into Britain by hook or by crook appear less than desirable—arose not from the law or from public policy or from administration but from those personal circumstances and accidents which cause, and always will cause, the fortunes and experience of one man to be different from another's.

But while to the immigrant entry to this country was admission to privileges and opportunities eagerly sought, the impact upon the existing population was very different. For reasons which they could not comprehend, and in pursuance of a decision by default, on which they were never consulted, they found themselves made strangers in their own country. They found their wives unable to obtain hospital beds in childbirth, their children unable to obtain school places, their homes and neighbourhoods changed beyond recognition, their plans and prospects for the future defeated; at work they found that employers hesitated to apply to the immigrant worker the standards of discipline and competence required of the native-born worker; they began to hear, as time went by, more and more voices which told them that they were now the unwanted. On top of this, they now learn that a one-way privilege is to be established by act of parliament; a law, which cannot, and is not intended, to operate to protect them or redress their grievances, is to be enacted to give the stranger, the disgruntled and the agent provocateur the power to pillory them for their private actions.

In the hundreds upon hundreds of letters I received when I last spoke on this subject two or three months ago, there was one striking feature which was largely new and which I find ominous. All Members of Parliament are used to the typical anonymous correspondent; but what surprised and alarmed me was the high proportion of ordinary, decent, sensible people, writing a rational and often well-educated letter, who believed that they had to omit their address because it was dangerous to have committed themselves to paper to a Member of Parliament agreeing with the views I had expressed, and that they would risk either penalties or reprisals if they were known to have done so. The sense of being a persecuted minority which is growing among ordinary English people in the areas of the country which are affected is something that those without direct experience can hardly imagine. I am going to allow just one of those hundreds of people to speak for

me. She did give her name and address, which I have
detached from the letter which I am about to read. She
was writing from Northumberland about something
which is happening at this moment in my own constituency:

'Eight years ago in a respectable street in Wolverhampton a house was sold to a negro. Now only one
white (a woman old-age pensioner) lives there. This
is her story. She lost her husband and both her sons
in the war. So she turned her seven-roomed house,
her only asset, into a boarding house. She worked hard
and did well, paid off her mortgage and began to put
something by for her old age. Then the immigrants
moved in. With growing fear, she saw one house after
another taken over. The quiet street became a place
of noise and confusion. Regretfully, her white tenants
moved out.

'The day after the last one left, she was awakened at
7 a.m. by two negroes who wanted to use her phone to
contact their employer. When she refused, as she would
have refused any stranger at such an hour, she was
abused and feared she would have been attacked but
for the chain on her door. Immigrant families have
tried to rent rooms in her house, but she always refused.
Her little store of money went, and after paying her
rates, she has less than £2 per week. She went to apply
for a rate reduction and was seen by a young girl,
who on hearing she had a seven-roomed house, suggested she should let part of it. When she said the only
people she could get were negroes, the girl said "racial
prejudice won't get you anywhere in this country". So
she went home.

'The telephone is her lifeline. Her family pay the bill, and help her out as best they can. Immigrants have offered to buy her house—at a price which the prospective landlord would be able to recover from his tenants in weeks, or at most a few months. She is becoming afraid to go out. Windows are broken. She finds excreta pushed through her letterbox. When she goes to the shops, she is followed by children, charming, wide-grinning piccaninnies. They cannot speak English, but one word they know. "Racialist", they chant. When the new Race Relations Bill is passed, this woman is convinced she will go to prison. And is she so wrong? I begin to wonder.'

The other dangerous delusion from which those who are wilfully or otherwise blind to realities suffer, is summed up in the word 'integration'. To be integrated into a population means to become for all practical purposes indistinguishable from its other members. Now, at all times, where there are marked physical differences, especially of colour, integration is difficult though, over a period, not impossible. There are among the Commonwealth immigrants who have come to live here in the last fifteen years or so, many thousands whose wish and purpose is to be integrated and whose every thought and endeavour is bent in that direction. But to imagine that such a thing enters the heads of a great and growing majority of immigrants and their descendants is a ludicrous misconception, and a dangerous one to boot.

We are on the verge here of a change. Hitherto it has been force of circumstance and of background which has rendered the very idea of integration in-

accessible to the greater part of the immigrant population—that they never conceived or intended such a
thing, and that their numbers and physical concentration meant the pressures towards integration which
normally bear upon any small minority did not operate.
Now we are seeing the growth of positive forces acting
against integration, of vested interests in the preservation and sharpening of racial and religious differences,
with a view to the exercise of actual domination, first
over fellow-immigrants and then over the rest of the
population. The cloud no bigger than a man's hand,
that can so rapidly overcast the sky, has been visible
recently in Wolverhampton and has shown signs of
spreading quickly. The words I am about to use, verba-
tim as they appeared in the local press on 17 February,
are not mine, but those of a Labour Member of Parliament who is a Minister in the present Government.
'The Sikh communities' campaign to maintain customs
inappropriate in Britain is much to be regretted.
Working in Britain, particularly in the public services,
they should be prepared to accept the terms and conditions of their employment. To claim special communal rights (or should they say rites?) leads to a
dangerous fragmentation within society. This commu-
nalism is a canker; whether practised by one colour or
another it is to be strongly condemned.' All credit to
John Stonehouse for having had the insight to perceive
that, and the courage to say it.

For these dangerous and divisive elements the legislation proposed in the Race Relations Bill is the very
pabulum they need to flourish. Here is the means of
showing that the immigrant communities can organise

to consolidate their members, to agitate and campaign against their fellow citizens, and to overawe and dominate the rest with the legal weapons which the ignorant and the ill-informed have provided. As I look ahead, I am filled with foreboding. Like the Roman, I seem to see 'the River Tiber foaming with much blood'. That tragic and intractable phenomenon which we watch with horror on the other side of the Atlantic but which there is interwoven with the history and existence of the States itself, is coming upon us here by our own volition and our own neglect. Indeed, it has all but come. In numerical terms, it will be of American proportions long before the end of the century. Only resolute and urgent action will avert it even now. Whether there will be the public will to demand and obtain that action, I do not know. All I know is that to see, and not to speak, would be the great betrayal.